# PADDLEFISH

# PADDLEFISH

*by*
CHRISTINE WARREN

DEPARTURE

Paddlefish

Departure Publishing LLC
PO Box 160818
Austin, TX 78716
(512) 347-8336
www.departurepublishing.com

First printing: October 2011

ISBN 10: 0983385726
ISBN 13: 9780983385721

Edited by Dave Lawton, Cazenovia, NY
Book design by Smashing Designs, La Jolla, CA
Photography by Team Paddlefish
Printed by The Sheridan Group, Ann Arbor, MI

The use of "Texas Water Safari" and "World's Toughest Boat Race" is with express permission of the Texas Water Safari Corporation. The opinions expressed in this book are those of the author and do not represent the views or opinions of the Texas Water Safari, it's officers or directors.

*This book is for Sophie, Tom, and my parents, Nancy and Duck.*
*Thank you all for keeping me afloat.*

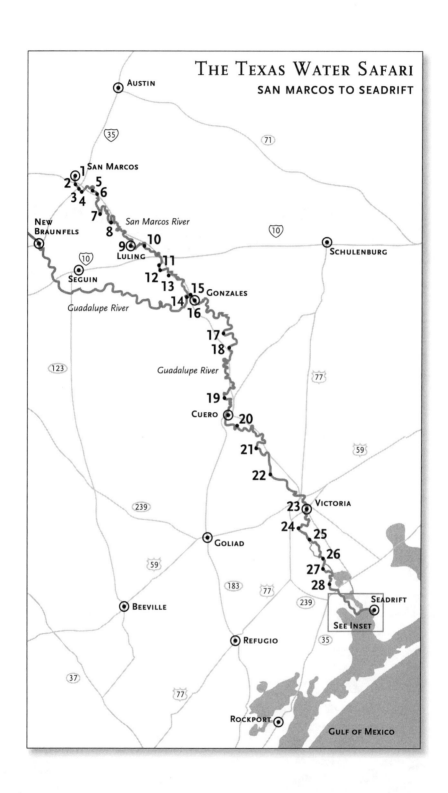

THE TEXAS WATER SAFARI
SAN MARCOS TO SEADRIFT

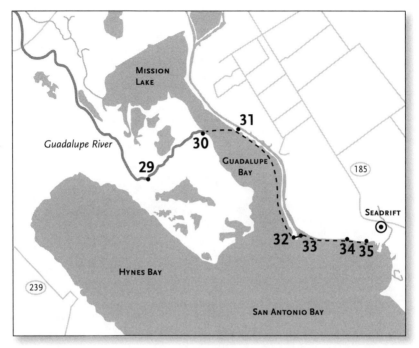

## LEGEND

# CONTENTS

# CHAPTER 1

# ON YOUR MARK, GET SET, JUST KIDDING

*"There cannot be a crisis today, my schedule is already full."*
– HENRY KISSINGER

*In an attempt to avoid eye contact with the teams on either side of me, I am looking down at my hands, which are wrapped firmly around my paddle. They look like bird feet perched on a swing inside a cage. Whose hands are these anyway? At some point during this strange journey, even my hands have become more athletic and lean.*

*To the right, to the left, and as far downriver as I can see, there is a bobbing and jabbering hodgepodge of paddlers and watercraft that have all signed on for a common goal. We have trained, prepared, and obsessed over this moment for months. Others before us have finished this race, so the goal is not insurmountable. Still, I can't help but notice the similarity between our milling, anxious mass, and a herd of cattle being led off to slaughter.*

*It's 8:35 a.m., and I'm trying to tune out the nervous, frenetic conversation that is passing back and forth across the front of my boat. The narrow, pointed bow of this canoe has been my home for many months. Over countless hours of paddle training, its foam-covered seat* and my rear-end have slowly melded into complimentary contours. My feet are pressing against the angled plate in the bow and my knees are wedged between the gunnels. I'm nestled in a familiar cocoon, and all the sights and sounds outside this cozy orbit are muted, almost as if I'm underwater.

My family and friends are gathered on the river banks, but I've already explained to them that I won't be waving, shouting, or throwing streamers like I'm boarding a luxury liner for some campy cruise. No doubt they have already noticed my out-of-character, antisocial behavior, but at least they know why.

Head bowed, I continue to hold my focus downward. Everyone handles anxiety differently and, right now, this is the best way I know to quietly stem the flow of adrenaline and calm the nervous boiling in my stomach. The paddlers around me probably think I'm taking a quick snooze, or praying, which is fine. But I'm not concerned with what others think of me at this particular moment. Over the past several years, I've learned to let go of the self-scrutinizing vanity that cares too much of what other people think. Some didn't think I could do this race; others didn't think I should. Those people didn't get me here and they're not here with me now.

It's 8:40 and the announcer is barking instructions over the scratchy PA system. The sun is topping the live oaks, and the humidity is oppressive.

Small rivulets of sweat are dripping down my back when the National Anthem starts at 8:52. I pretend to join the others in a show of patriotism while I struggle to maintain my fabricated calm. The butterflies in my stomach have morphed into an angry mob. My heart is pounding in my chest. Blood is coursing and converging through the veins in my hands; they look like an aerial map of the rivers that I'm about to explore. I take a long, deep breath and loosen the grip on my paddle.

It's 8:59. I'm sitting up tall, stretching my back and scanning *the riverbank for my support team. The announcer has his pistol in the air. Voices are counting in concert...6...5...4...3...2...1...*

———

A clap of thunder shook my house and jolted me from a deep sleep. I sat up and stared at the alarm clock, waiting for the numbers to come into focus.

3:07 a.m.

A brilliant flash illuminated my bedroom, followed immediately by another roar of thunder. The rain came down in sheets and I thought about the river as I slipped back to sleep.

*Good...we could use some extra water flow...*

———

I awoke the next morning, Wednesday, June 9th, with less than three days to finish gearing up for the race. I spent most of the day running around Austin with my ten-year-old daughter, Sophie, and buying the remaining items on our list: Clif gels, electrolyte powders, protein bars, first aid supplies, batteries. Lots of stores, lots of stops and not much time.

By 4:00 p.m. I was beginning to wear down. I had been battling bronchitis for over a week and the medications combined with the heat and humidity were sapping my energy levels. The streets swarming with impatient motorists weren't helping matters. Afternoon traffic in Austin, Texas is always selfish warfare, but today it seemed especially unbearable.

While stalled against my will at an unreasonably long traffic light, my mind wandered off in protest. For a few stolen moments, harried thoughts of my to-do list melted away and left a perfectly blank slate. Suddenly my phone rang out like a shot through the quiet of my car and rocked me back to reality. At the exact same time a car honked from behind me, and Sophie urgently announced, "Mommy! The light is green!"

Frazzled, I grabbed for my ringing phone while I wheeled left through the intersection using up the final seconds of the protected green arrow and irritating the drivers stacked up behind me in the turn lane.

I looked at the display on my phone: BANNING.

*Finally!*

I was already talking as I answered, "Where have you been? I've been trying to call you all afternoon!"

"I know, sorry. Just trying to tie up loose ends before the race."

Banning Collins is a fly-fishing guide, sales rep and dear friend who, about a year ago, agreed to be my partner in the Texas Water Safari. Since our first training run in September 2009, we had quite literally covered a lot of ground together. Hundreds of river and road miles, thousands upon thousands of paddle strokes, snakes, bleeding palms, mysterious rashes, angry geese, low hanging tree limbs that capsized our boat, logjams, heartburn, dehydration, biting cold and blistering heat. There were countless hours of laughing in the boat and free therapy time on each other's love life. Now we were drowning in the final stages of our preparation and counting down the hours to race day.

"Banning, I'm worried about the rainstorm that came through last night."

"Oh, we'll be fine. It'll just make the river faster."

"No, I've been looking at the race discussion board online. There's talk of a delay."

Ever optimistic, he said, "There won't be a delay. The water from last night's storm will move down ahead of us. We still have three days. The river will be fine."

"Well, they said the Safari Board is posting a decision tomorrow at the latest."

"It'll be fine. Let's keep going with what we have to do. The race will happen."

"I hope you're right. I've got a couple more stops and then I'll check the race board again when I get home to see if there's any news."

A coughing fit seized my chest so I reached for the inhaler and sucked in a dose of calm. I was sick of this infection and desperate to get well before the race. When we finished our errands, Sophie and I returned home to fix dinner and organize gear.

At around 8 p.m. I hit the refresh button on my browser and saw the following post:

*The Texas Water Safari board has selected to postpone the race scheduled for this Saturday, June 12th 2010, due to predicted flood stage water at several race checkpoints on the lower river including Cuero 236, Victoria City Park and the Saltwater Barrier. The race will be rescheduled for Saturday July 10th 2010. More details about the race postponement will be published tomorrow.*

My heart sank and I could feel my chest tightening up. I read the post again, and then I read a few of the replies. This couldn't be happening.

The rainstorm that came late Tuesday night was a freak event. The weather forecasters were calling for scattered showers and everyone involved with the Texas Water Safari was hoping for a water boost; just enough rain to increase the river flows on the San Marcos and the Guadalupe, but not enough to make things dangerous.

Little did we know.

New Braunfels, Texas got thirteen inches of rain in two hours and there was catastrophic flooding in the upper Guadalupe watershed. Businesses were destroyed, homes were flooded, and one person in a riverside campground was swept away. The TV newscasters called it a "rain bomb." Areas to the north and south of New Braunfels only got an inch or two.

I stood for a moment and stared at the computer screen. Was this a bad dream? For the next few minutes I paced around my house in an emotional daze. I stopped and stared at the carefully arranged piles of food, clothing, and race gear in my living room, but that only made me feel worse. There were dozens of phone calls that needed to be made—quickly—but I didn't want to pick up the phone and make it real.

I kept telling myself to keep it all in perspective, someone had died in the flood. I felt guilty being so depressed about the race, but I couldn't have predicted the emotional and psychological blow this delay would have on me. The Texas Water Safari had only been postponed twice in its 47-year history, in 2004 it was actually postponed a second time within the same summer. I couldn't even wrap my head around that thought.

How in the world would I continue training for this? I wanted to be done with training—I *was* done, dammit! We had peaked on our paddle runs three weeks out and had tapered off. How would we ramp back up and taper down again in a month?

At that point my mind began racing through all of the people and travel and logistics involved in this crazy race. What about my parents who were flying in from Montana? They'd have to change their flights and hotel reservations. And, Tom, my boyfriend? He was coming in from Mobile. What about my girlfriends from Alabama who had rented a van to drive out and follow the race? What about all of the motel rooms that we've booked along the race route in Gonzales, Cuero, Victoria and Seadrift? I would have to cancel my annual two-week fishing trip to Montana. That thought alone made me nauseous.

And Sophie!

She'll be in summer camp on the new start date and I won't be able to pick her up on visitor's day. My head started pounding and I could feel another coughing fit coming on.

I picked up my phone to call Banning. He didn't answer so I left him a message to ring me back as soon as possible. Next, I scrolled through my contacts to "Tosh Brown." This was going to be painful, but I couldn't put it off.

"Bad news," I said.

"You're kidding…"

"I wish I was. The Safari Board just posted it on the website."

"When's the make-up date?"

"Saturday July 10th."

Tosh was silent for a few seconds. "Christine, that's the day I leave for Alaska."

"I know, this is awful."

Tosh had booked this trip a year ago. It was his son's high school graduation present. They were scheduled for a week of fly fishing at a small lodge and wouldn't be able to rebook during the prime summer season.

"I'm sorry," he said, "but that takes me out…"

Tosh was our team captain, and he had also invested a year of his life in this race. Granted, he hadn't put in the actual paddling miles, but he had built our website, shot hundreds of photographs, attended all of the preliminary races and scouting runs, and he had memorized the bankside perspective of the entire race route. Tosh was our logistical lifeline and now we would have to replace him.

"We'll find someone else," I told him. "We'll have to, there's no other choice. Maybe Tom or my dad can do it…maybe there'll be other teams that can't race, so maybe *their* team captains will be available?"

We talked for a bit longer and Tosh apologized, again, and

said that he'd do whatever he could to help train a new team captain before July 10th. I could tell that he was crushed about missing the race.

I sat down at my desk and began making a list. I am the queen of lists, not just making them, but conquering them with a vengeance, one task at a time. Nothing happens if it's not on my list. At the top of this new and depressing page I wrote "Get new team captain".

As I sat trying to organize my thoughts, my mind kept racing through dozens of scenarios. *What if it keeps raining? What if they postpone the race again? What if they cancel it altogether? Oh my word, what about my fundraising?*

My friend Anna Luce's daughter has an aggressive and virtually unknown disease called Rett Syndrome and I had set a goal to raise $5,000, as well as awareness to help fight the disease. This commitment and responsibility fueled me during training when I would have rather lounged on the couch instead of hitting the gym, or when I wanted to devour an entire pizza instead of six-ounces of roasted vegetables. In a horribly depressed economy I had already coerced friends and companies into making personal donations and sponsoring our team.

*I don't have to give the money back, do I? How does that work?*

I wrote all these issues down as bullet points on my new and ever-growing list. Then I got up from my desk and walked back to the living room and stood staring at the piles of gear.

*This race HAS to happen…it's taken a lot of time and money to pull all of this together…*

The phone rang; it was Banning again. I delivered the bad news, and he logged on to the website to see the post with his own eyes. I vented about my dread of continued training, the pain of re-scheduling dozens of people, and Tosh's travel conflict and having to find a new team captain. He commiserated with each point and then quietly he inserted, "Christine…I'm supposed to be out of town that week."

I paused briefly and then continued chattering on about the to-do list, rescheduling flights, more training runs, and a new team captain.

Looking back, I obviously dismissed the significance of Banning's statement.

# CHAPTER 2

# THE WORLD'S TOUGHEST BOAT RACE

*"There's a lot of blood, sweat and guts between dreams and success."*

– PAUL "BEAR" BRYANT

The Texas Water Safari is one of those rare events that boasts an authenticity truly greater than its lore. Since 1963 the race has run continually for forty-seven years. For those of you keeping score, that's three years longer than the Super Bowl.

The Safari begins in San Marcos on the southern rim of the Texas Hill Country and ends in the sleepy coastal fishing village of Seadrift. As the crow flies, the two towns are only 125 miles apart. By river it's a 260-mile twisting and winding riparian ass kicking that must be completed in 100 hours or less. There are twelve checkpoints along the route and each of those comes with a cutoff time. If you miss a cutoff, you're out, even if it's the first checkpoint—even if you only miss it by a matter of minutes.

The race was originally founded by Frank Brown and Big Willie George of San Marcos. In the early 1960's Brown worked for the San Marcos Chamber of Commerce and had a hunch that the river could be a bigger recreational attraction for the city. George owned a local burger joint called Big Willie's Hamburgers and was an avid outdoorsman. At a local archery event Brown asked George if anyone had ever taken a boat from Aquarena Springs to the Gulf of Mexico. No one could recall such a voyage ever happening, so the two decided to do it themselves.

In 1962 Brown and George took a 12-foot semi V-hull row boat from San Marcos to Corpus Christi, an estimated 400 mile trip that took them almost 30 days to complete. They fished and hunted for their food, accepted only the rare candy bar from strangers on bridges, and slept in a pup tent to avoid snakes. They each lost approximately 40 pounds on the voyage.

Deciding that others should experience their adventure, they created the first ever Texas Water Safari one year later. Racers traveled from Aquarena Springs (the current starting line of the Safari) to Corpus Christi (about 140 miles longer than the current race route). LIFE Magazine published an article on the first race in June 1963. Fifty-seven boats started at the headwaters of the San Marcos River; photos from the LIFE Magazine article show paddlers in pith helmets with life jackets tied around their necks. When the race finished twelve days later, only two teams had reached the finish line in Corpus Christi.

Legend has it that one massive logjam they encountered near the end of the race required a four-mile portage through snake infested marshes. One competitor was quoted as saying, "I was praying a snake would bite me so I could get out of this thing honorably."

Joe Passant and his partner made it through the harrowing four-mile logjam but realized they had dwindling food supplies as they faced the final bay crossing. Clif Bars weren't available back then, so they caught and ate a stingray instead.

Most of the boats that reached the bay faltered. Some boats had sails but their captains were poor seamen. Others that didn't have sails simply couldn't handle the 35 mph headwind and four-foot swells. One racer who didn't finish praised the four who did when he said, "They had to be a bunch of real mean critters." One of the four who persevered to the finish line said his team made it on "blood, blisters and blasphemy."

Just as it was in 1963, The Texas Water Safari is still a self-sustaining race, which means that paddlers must start with every-thing they'll need in the way of clothing, food, emergency gear, boat repair materials, etc. The team captains can replenish their paddlers with water and ice at each of the checkpoints—but that's it. Nothing else. No cheeseburgers, no Advil, no red wine. No bandages, no duct tape, not even a zip tie. Nothing.

The team captains are also required to log in their paddlers at each checkpoint with the race officials. They live in their trucks, napping in folding chairs like bums under bridges or whatever scant shade they can find. Not knowing when their team might arrive at a checkpoint, they scramble from one to the next and then perch on the banks, waiting. At the end of the race they often smell just as bad as the paddlers.

It's up to each team captain whether they handle their duties alone, or with a support crew. Most of the paddling teams have an en-tourage of friends and family members that follow them downriver, but there's one additional hard and fast rule.

*No one*, besides the designated team captain is allowed to as-sist the racers in any way. The team captains can hand the racers wa-ter and ice, and the racers can hand back their trash and empty water jugs. But *no one*, not even the team captain, can touch the boat or the racers. No hugs, no high-fives, and no flying chest bumps (until the finish line). They can cheer and encourage all they want, but no physical contact is permitted.

With ten different classifications, such as solo, tandem and novice, the field of entrants in the Texas Water Safari is as diverse as the terrain that they paddle. Some are in it to win their divisions and those hardcore racers will typically attempt to run the course non-stop with only brief pauses at the checkpoints for water and ice. They don't sleep, they barely eat, and they pee in their boats. The record finishing time occurred in 1997 by a six-man team that completed the race in 29 hours and 46 minutes. The math alone on that one is mind-boggling.

Others enter the race only with the hope of finishing or making a respectable showing. In years of ample rainfall and good water flows, up to 75% of the teams will finish within the 100-hour allotment. In dry years, the sandbars and logjams and portages will eliminate the majority of the novices and a good many veteran paddlers, as well.

The race is unofficially divided into three distinct segments: the San Marcos River, the Guadalupe River, and Guadalupe Bay. The starting line straddles the spring-fed headwaters of the San Marcos River, which flows 81 miles southeast before it pours into the Guadalupe River just above the town of Gonzales. The Guadalupe River originates in the Texas Hill Country west of Kerrville, but the race only covers its final 173 miles before it strains through a marshy delta into Guadalupe Bay. The final segment is the shortest, only six paddling miles, but that quick sprint across the bay to the finish line in Seadrift is the least predictable. Damaged boats, blasting winds, crashing waves, injury, sleep deprivation, and fatigue have claimed many teams in the bay, literally within sight of the finish line.

The race is held each year in June, apparently to maximize the torture from the Texas heat and accentuate the lack of daily hygiene. Space and weight are limited in race boats so luxuries like toothpaste, soap and deodorant rarely make the cut. Most paddlers (and some team captains) are left to marinate in their own human brine.

Paddling a canoe for an hour or two on a 100-degree afternoon with 80% humidity is not easy. Paddling for four days in those conditions is a physical and mental torment that words can barely do justice. And if the number of river miles between the start and finish aren't reason enough not to enter this race, one must also consider the number of portages where racers must carry their canoes over and around concrete dams, sandbars and logjams. While the physical barriers are daunting, the cadre of Old Testament flora and fauna that Mother Nature dials up is what truly sets this race apart: rattlesnakes, fire ants, jellyfish, alligators, cactus, spiders, thorn brush, water moccasins, bull nettle, wasps, poison ivy, feral hogs, swarms of mosquitoes—and everyone's favorite parasite, Giardia.

It's no wonder *Forbes* magazine once listed the Texas Water Safari as one of the world's ten toughest endurance races. Included in that list were the Iditarod and the Badwater Death Valley Ultramarathon.

When I first started researching this race, I naively dismissed most of the warnings as macho hyperbole. But after a year of training and countless discussions with Safari veterans, I'm now convinced that they may have actually understated this hellish undertaking.

There have been actual snake bites and wasp attacks. People have succumbed to simultaneous vomiting and diarrhea. Racers have lost their headlamps to airborne alligator gar in the middle of the night. Paddlers have been found wandering the riverbanks naked and speaking in tongues. One contestant was so elated to reach the finish line that he did a celebratory swan dive back into the bay and was promptly stung by a stingray.

Other tales are less sensational, but equally rattling. I met a paddler during our training who had to quit the race because the intensity of his bow light bothered his eyes so badly while paddling at night that he couldn't stop vomiting. Other teams have been taken out by submerged stumps that gashed their boats, or concussions caused by low-hanging limbs. Countless teams have reported getting lost or taking wrong turns that cost them hours and jeopardized their cutoff times at checkpoints. At first I questioned how in the world one could get lost on a river, isn't it just a line of water running downhill?

Apparently not.

The upper watershed is pretty straightforward from a naviga-tion perspective, but the coastal delta is laced with channels and lakes and marshes that all look the same, especially in the middle of the night after a few days without sleep.

In the 47-year history of the Texas Water Safari, no one has died during the actual race, but a paddler did die during a practice run at Ottine Dam. It was a father-son team and they apparently mis-judged their approach to the dam during extremely high water flow. The current pulled them over the top and into the roiling hydraulic below the dam. The son managed to swim to safety but, sadly, his father didn't survive.

When I first heard about The Texas Water Safari I appraised it as a gathering of competitive lunatics all driven by the common goal of conquering a nasty stretch of water in an impossibly short period of time, during the exact *wrong* season of the year. I never paid much attention to the actual prizes given to the finishers and divisional winners, but given the amount of torture they were will-ing to endure, I assumed that the rewards were substantial. Why else would someone sign up for such a god-awful race?

At some point during my yearlong odyssey of research and preparation I confirmed the unexpected answer to that seemingly ra-tional question. After months of training, after huge outlays of cash, after time away from family and friends and days of suffering on the water, all in the slightly misguided spirit of adventure and competi-tion, Safari finishers are awarded…a patch.

That's right. A three-inch diameter swatch of cheaply stitched cloth. No money, no cruise vacations, no fancy gift certificates, no sponsored trips to Disney World.

*A flippin' PATCH?*

*Are you kidding me?*

I wanted one.

# CHAPTER 3

# ADRIFT

*"It is not best to swap horses while crossing the river."*
—ABRAHAM LINCOLN

I poked my wrist out from beneath the comforter to check my watch. 1:52 pm.

*They'll be here in less than ten minutes...*

It was Thursday afternoon, June 10th, and Banning and Tosh were coming over to discuss the delay and plans for the make-up race. Unfortunately, Tosh would also be handing over his binders, maps, GPS, video camera, SPOT Tracker, and a year's worth of vested time and interest in this project.

I was thoroughly depressed and deflated by the race delay, and even though it was a gorgeous summer day, I spent most of it watching movies in bed with Sophie. We must have been on our third DVD by that point, but I hadn't paid a lick of attention to any of them. I had been listless all day, completely overwhelmed with the news of last night and thoroughly flummoxed on how to piece together a new set of logistics.

Having to find a new team captain was a blow, but it was possible. I had been on the phone well into the night and all morning trying to rearrange layers of details. In lieu of other candidates, my dad and Tom had already offered to step in as team captains, but we all agreed it would be ideal if we could find someone who had either captained before or had a modicum of experience with the race.

While no one had ever officially nominated me team secretary, it had been my role for the past year so instinctively I printed out three copies of my new list of logistics to be discussed.

Banning and Tosh arrived as planned and we all took time to vent about this terrible stroke of bad luck. If only the rains had been ten miles to the north or south, we'd be fine. While the worst of the flooding had been on the upper Guadalupe, above the race route, the officials were concerned, wisely, that the bubble of floodwater would travel downriver and arrive in Victoria about the time early racers were reaching that checkpoint. I couldn't help but picture a snake eating a rat, and the image of the bulge as the rat moved through the snake's body.

From the officials' standpoint, it was a safety issue, plain and simple. We understood, but that didn't stop us from bitching and moaning about the irony of it all. Texas had been in a drought for two years. The 2009 Water Safari was one of the most grim in history with trickle flows and only about half of the boats reaching the finish line in Seadrift. We'd been praying for rain for a year.

Apparently we over-prayed.

Suddenly I was sick of bellyaching; it was time to move forward. I handed out copies of my printout and walked Banning and Tosh through all of the details I'd thought of, including the hunt for a new team captain, a revised training schedule, a night paddling run, and support team logistics. I ran through the list, along with my suggestions, and asked where we should go from here.

Nervous and reticent, Banning reacted innocuously to my list, ultimately changing the direction of the whole conversation when he simply said, "I have a conflict."

*A conflict. Wait…what? Did he say conflict?*

Banning went on to explain that he had two work trips during the week of July 10th, and that he planned to talk to his clients to see if he could reschedule. Tosh and I threw out every possible scenario, trying to help him find a way to make it work, but we both knew that the decision was ultimately his.

Digging deep, I shook off the cultish, brainwashing grip that the Safari had on me and tried to see it from a well-adjusted person's point of view. Quietly I offered, "Banning, this race isn't meant to ruin our professional lives."

I said it. And I earnestly meant it. But I was also swirling in a firestorm of thoughts and emotions. I was upset. I was shocked. In my wildest imagination, my taxed brain could not process the notion of dropping out of this race after such a long, grinding year of preparation and training.

Banning asked if he could take the weekend to think it over, so we wrapped up the meeting and they gathered their things to leave.

After he and Tosh left I crawled back in bed with Sophie and cried enough tears to re-flood the Guadalupe. My eyes were burning, my head was spinning, and my stomach churned. Thankfully, Tom was scheduled to arrive from Mobile the next day. Without that deadline to force me out of the house, I'm fairly certain I would have stayed in bed the entire weekend.

A few hours before Tom's scheduled arrival, I decided that it was time to stop focusing on the negative.

"Sophie, Mommy is about to teach you one of the most important lessons of your whole life. I want you to remember this forever. When you are blue, and life seems like it's pinning you down, there is always one thing that lifts your spirits and gets you going."

"Prayer?"

Okay, so apparently I had already taught her at least *one* good lesson, but that's not where I was headed at that particular moment.

"Well, yes, prayer is of course the most important. But also… never forget…. music!"

I tossed her a hairbrush microphone, grabbed a bottle of shampoo to sing into myself, and cranked the iPod speakers as loud as they would go. With ABBA blaring throughout the bathroom, we sang and danced and got ready to pick up Tom at the airport.

Sophie was a super trooper all day and Tom was a godsend. He served as a human guardrail, gently guiding me back into the sane lane each time I drifted off to get angry, or sink into another funk. At one point on Friday evening I retreated to my bedroom and he found me back there, despondent and weepy.

"Am I being punished? Is it because I've spent too much time on this—time away from Sophie? Did I push the race too much? Was I too aggressive in my fundraising? I think God is angry at me for having too much hubris. Maybe I'm being punished because my life is going so well and I've got you and Sophie and our future and everything I've ever wanted, and I'm being punished because I don't deserve it."

Tom hugged me, "No, Christine, come on. That's not it at all. All the racers are going through the same thing. There are a lot of people thrown out of whack from this delay. It's just Mother Nature. It's gonna work out. I bet Banning does the race. He's not going to walk away from a year of such hard work. He's just figuring out how to make it happen."

I was in awe of how many of my friends and relatives instinctively registered with the psychological body slam of this race delay. Emails of support were pouring in. Some were quoting scripture, and others were quoting famous athletes.

My uncle drew a touching comparison to Muhammad Ali's much-hyped Rumble in The Jungle which after months of preparation and crescendo, was delayed a month when Ali's opponent, George Foreman, suffered a cut over his eye while training. The world stage, the press, and Ali himself, had to wait for Foreman's injury to heal. Ali was in Zaire, hoping for his shot, but instead of letting the ambiguity and limbo eat away at him, he seemed to gain strength from the delay. He worked the international press into a veritable frenzy, and when he finally made it into the ring, he knocked out Foreman in the eighth round.

But I'm not "The Greatest". I'm not even sure I'm great. I'm just a single mom knocking on the door of forty. I measure a run on the treadmill not by miles, but by three or four songs on the iPod. And while I knew this race would call for a huge dose of perseverance, I thought it would happen on the river. I had no idea how much would be required before we ever put the boat in the water.

On Saturday morning I was feeling better so the three of us decided to take a leisurely drive. Since we were supposed to be racing that morning, I decided to show Sophie and Tom where the Water Safari starts and a few other key points along the upper river.

The city of San Marcos, thirty miles south of Austin, is the county seat for Hays County, named for Tennessee transplant John Coffee Hays. Hays was one of the early Texas Rangers, known for his successful raids against the Comanches in West Texas. I'm not sure if the town was named for the river, or vice versa, but many historians claim that the spring-fed San Marcos River boasts the earliest known accounts of human civilization in North America. Early Texas settlers dammed the river in multiple places for cotton gins and to leverage the fertility of its flow, so I guess I have them to thank for all of the portages.

I showed Tom and Sophie the ramp at City Park where we'd put the boat in so many times for training runs. The clarity of the water in this part of the river is mesmerizing and because of its purity, the headwaters were established in the 1950's as a tourist attraction called Aquarena Springs. For decades, the main attraction at Aquarena Springs was a swimming pig that delighted crowds with acts of waterborne daring. The original swimming swine was named "Magnolia," but after her passing she was replaced by "Ralph." Apparently "Ralph the Swimming Pig" had a nice ring to it, or perhaps it was easier to fit on the billboards up and down IH-35. That name stuck to all subsequent pigs until 1996 when the act was eventually shelved.

From City Park, we drove to Rio Vista Dam, a sluice-box rapid that is always an entertaining bumper car cluster on race day. Tom was fascinated by everything I showed him. Having studied the mileage spreadsheets, the checkpoint list, GPS coordinates and Google Earth images of the race route for almost year, he was finally seeing it all with his own eyes.

So we kept going.

I showed them Staples Dam, the first checkpoint of the race and a considerable portage. Further down river we stopped to look at the Westerfield low water crossing, the first place that Banning and I ever launched on our training runs on the San Marcos.

I showed them the Martindale Dam and low water crossing where we had limboed flat on our backs under the concrete bridge with scant inches of daylight between the bridge deck and an involuntary breast reduction. No one ever said this was a safe race.

We pushed further south toward Luling and then to the third checkpoint at Palmetto State Park, and finally the dam at Gonzales, which is just below the point where the San Marcos River pours into the Guadalupe.

Spurred into a historical narrative by all that she had seen on this day, Sophie spent most of the ride back to Austin sharing nuggets of Texana from each of the towns we had visited. Apparently, she had paid attention in her fourth grade Texas History class.

Halfway home, we stopped in Lockhart, known as "The Barbecue Capital of Texas," and picked up a heaping pile of beef brisket and trimmings from Kreuz's Market. During the months of training I had eaten very little red meat, opting instead for spinach-chia smoothies, organic apple chicken sausage, and other benign delicacies. But what the hell? Now I had another month until the race, right? Why not indulge?

Bad idea.

In the middle of night, my stomach launched a Texas-scale revolution against the pile of smoked beef and barbecue sauce that I had inhaled at dinner. By morning I was feeling a little better, but still kind of woozy when I heard the chime on my phone as we were heading out the door to church. It was a text message from Banning, "Can we talk?"

Later that afternoon I met Banning at a coffee shop and listened calmly as he explained that he couldn't do the race. I had trouble processing his decision, but I had to respect it. The Texas Water Safari is not the type of activity that you coerce someone into doing. We would be marginalized, at best, if one half of a two-person team wasn't fully onboard.

I walked through my kitchen door and found Tom and Sophie anxiously awaiting my return. I shook my head to indicate Banning's decision of "no."

Tom scooped me up in a big hug and Sophie piled on.

# CHAPTER 4

# DOES THIS CANOE MAKE MY BUTT LOOK BIG?

*"The biggest myth about Southern women is that we are frail types, fainting on our sofas...nobody where I grew up ever acted like that. We were about as fragile as coal trucks."*
– LEE SMITH

Since my announcement that I'd be racing in the Texas Water Safari for a cause, I received a good bit of television and print press about my quest for the coveted patch. While those interviews allowed me to talk about Rett Syndrome, which helped my fundraising goals, I was also thrown a few questions and comments that caught me a bit off guard. At the end of an interview with Pamela LeBlanc of the *Austin American Statesman*, she said, "You just don't seem like the kind of person to do something like this. You seem like such a girlie-girl."

Immediately after that interview I was picking up Sophie from school when the mother of one of her friends said, "I just love your outfits. You always look so casual and outdoorsy."

I recognize that stereotypes exist, but the older I get the harder it is for me to stay put in mine—and the fact that I'd signed up for a 260-mile canoe race added to the confusion.

A few days before the original race date, I did a video interview with my friend Tim Cole from Austin. Tim works in advertising and had been following my training and preparation with the plan of producing a documentary on the Safari. He would be following us from start to finish during the race, but he first wanted to get some back story.

As we settled into my living room with the video camera rolling, Tim fired off one of those seemingly innocuous questions that's really tough to answer on cue.

"So, Christine, why don't you start by telling me who you are…"

I answered with a perfunctory light response, glazing over more complicated and winding answers. It's hard to explain in a sound bite, but to look back at my life in sequence it makes sense to me how I've arrived, quite organically, at this place where labels don't apply, or adhere, as cleanly as they once did.

I was born in September 1970 in Nashville, Tennessee while my parents were finishing up at Vanderbilt University. When I was about a year old we moved to Dallas, Texas where I have deep family roots on my mother's side, Daughters of the Texas Revolution, and all that. When I was nine we moved to London where my father worked in the banking business. When I was twelve we moved back to Dallas, then almost immediately back to Nashville where I stayed through high school. From there I trotted off to college in Chapel Hill, North Carolina where I folded right in with the Bourbon & Coke crowd and cheered on the Tarheels among a sea of blue blazers and darling dresses.

After college, I moved back to Dallas for my first job; I was an Assistant Buyer at Neiman-Marcus. My ex-husband and I actually met at Neiman's (he worked in the marketing department) and after a whirlwind courtship, we were married. From there we moved to Boston where he went to business school. Sophie was born soon after our arrival in Boston, but we eventually moved to Austin where all of his University of Texas undergrad friends lived.

Austin is a city with a delightfully schizophrenic character; a place where you can observe traditional family values and still be wildly creative. It's an eclectic stew of activity, a town that will keep you young forever.

Unfortunately, despite all the charms of our new hometown, our marriage eventually unraveled and ultimately ended in 2004. Some people say divorce is a gift, of sorts. Those are probably the same dingdongs whose mothers and grandmothers call getting their period "The Gift." For the record, I don't remember registering for either. For me, divorce was more like a wakeup call, a time to rise up and see what this once-cheeky southern bird was made of. Cheese grits or true grit? Turns out it was a hearty helping of both.

Any way you serve it up, I am a part of the places I've lived and all the moves I've made. Other than my brief detours to Britain and the Northeast, Texas and the South have long been at odds within my heart. It's juke joints and chicken biscuits versus honkytonks and breakfast tacos. I listen to soul music and western swing; I shag and I two-step. Texas offers a new frontier where anyone can become a hero or a millionaire, while southern families are rooted in tradition, natural extensions of the old storied homes they inherit and inhabit.

Even though I was born in The South, I'm not really sure if I fit the traditional Southern Girl profile. Early on I sensed that brains and brass would take me on a slightly different track. I was probably even a bit smug in the fact that I operated outside that stereotype.

Or did I?

I attended an all-girls high school with saddle oxfords and plaid kilt uniforms. Our mascot was a Honeybear, but I was on the riflery team. I wasn't a very good Junior Leaguer but I was a darn good Rush Chair for my sorority. I was never a husband-hunter, but I did marry quite young. I've never played down my smarts around a man, but I am an awfully good flirt.

If forced to choose, I suppose Texas honkytonks and breakfast tacos would win out. I've been in Austin for ten years now and, surprisingly, have lived in my current house longer than any other home in my entire thirty-nine year history. Despite moving away several times, I always seem to find my way back to the Lone Star State. So certainly I must be a Texan, right?

Texas, Southern...girlie girl, tomboy...tomato, tomah-to, potato, pot-tahto. All I know is that I was exactly two things: a mom, and a woman mildly obsessed with a 260-mile canoe race, who may have sacrificed way too much in the past year in order to complete it. I was run down, amped up, eager to celebrate at the finish line, ready to enjoy some red wine and stay up late with friends. I was dying to wear a dress again instead of paddling clothes. I had sworn off heels for fear of injury and I was sick to death of flats and flip-flops. I was distracted, drained, excited and inspired by some incredibly big life conversations I'd been having with my boyfriend, Tom, about our future.

More than anything, though, I was craving time with Sophie, time just to be "Mommy" for a little while. Not paddler, not novice, not underdog...just Mommy.

# CHAPTER 5

# PERSEVERANCE LOOKS A LOT LIKE CRAZY

*"We will either find a way, or make one."*
—HANNIBAL

One reason that I love rivers is they are always moving forward. Lakes suffer from inertia; oceans and their tides are so complicated. But rivers just press on and move ahead. Their flows rise and fall, their energy levels undulate, but they are always charging onward, unceasing in their goal to reach the coast.

I shared the same goal.

On Monday morning, June 14th, I awoke with refreshed resolve. While I momentarily found myself picking through my race map and wondering where we might be paddling were it not for a Biblical flood, I quickly shelved those pangs of self pity and refocused my efforts on rebuilding my race team.

While my bronchitis was better, I was still experiencing the occasional hacking cough outburst. If there was any silver lining at all with this postponement, it would have to be the four extra weeks to clear my lungs. I put that on my mental list of advantages, it was time to think positive and get down to business.

Banning was out, and I needed a new partner. I didn't have time to wax poetic about what we'd accomplished together or how and why this had happened. Monday morning kicked me into business mode and I was relentless. The night before, I had actually considered paddling solo, even though only ten women had ever completed the race in that classification. Thankfully, Tom caught me and yanked me away from that cliff's edge before I leaned out too far. So, if racing solo wasn't an option, then I basically had two choices: find a new partner, or an intact team who needed to fill an empty seat in their canoe.

I emailed every Safari veteran, friend, mentor, and acquaintance I had come to know in the past year. I was shameless. I even emailed the Chairman of the Board of the Texas Water Safari. I never heard back from him, but I did get a response from every other person that I contacted. It was very touching and quite humbling, and their replies all brought the same encouragement: don't give up… other people are looking, too…we'll let you know if we hear anything.

After the email barrage, I set about crafting a post for the Paddle24seven message board. At first I started off humble and reserved, but then I decided to hang it all out there. At that point I had nothing to lose.

First, I explained the basic circumstances: novice paddler, trained in an aluminum canoe, needing a teammate. From there I went in to a bit more detail: I had trained for a year, and the majority of that time I paddled in the bow. I raced in two of the Town Lake Prelims and the forty-mile Texas Water Safari Prelim. I had completed eight of the twelve race segments including the crucial bay to finish line stretch. I had paddled the tough segments of the San Marcos River numerous times, and several of them during high, dangerous flows. Three weeks before the original race, I had done a brutal three-day 110-mile training run in 95-degree weather. And finally, to sweeten the deal, I listed all of the gear that was currently stacked in my living room: packaged food, water jugs, life vests, emergency gear, boat repair kit, GPS (programmed), SPOT Tracker, headlights and batteries, extra drinking tubes, etc. At the end of the post, I signed off with the following:

> *Oh, and I like pina coladas and getting caught in the rain. Or, not, if you don't. Either way...I just want to race in the Safari.*

> *Many Thanks!*
> *Christine*

For the next half-hour, I sat in front of my computer, hitting refresh and watching to see if anyone had viewed my post. Zero, zero zero. Wait...one view...then two views! So where were the responses? Why wasn't my phone ringing off the hook?

My phone did ring a few times that morning. My dad nobly called and offered to race with me. It was very sweet, but given that he hadn't trained, didn't know the rivers, and would be in Montana up until the race, that wasn't really a viable option. Later, a friend called and said he knew a guy named Mike from his gym who was really fit. He had taken the liberty of asking him if he'd consider doing something like this, and Mike from the Gym replied, "Sure, what the hell."

His reply wasn't really that different than Banning's many months ago when I first asked him to do this race, but at this stage of the game I needed more conviction. And experience.

This was going to be even harder than I realized. I had never done the race, but having spent a year preparing and ten months actively training, I already knew what non-Safari people had a difficult time grasping: physical fitness and strength simply aren't enough. I needed someone who had done the race before. Or had trained on these rivers, or at least rivers like them. This was a serious long shot.

I had to break away from obsessively staring at my computer screen. I ran a few errands, nervously cleaned the house, did a few loads of laundry. Finally, around 3 p.m., I received an email that caused my spirits to soar. My friend Debbie Richardson who was racing on a three-person woman's team called The Hippie Chicks emailed and said, "Have you found a partner? Don't say yes to anyone until you speak with me. I may have someone."

Her friend Phil Meyer had seen my post and called her to see if I was the real deal. She vouched for me.

*Hallelujah!*

Phil called and we had a great conversation. He had done the Safari in 2009 with a five-man boat that actually finished in 12th place. He was an avid paddle racer, worked at the Texas Rowing Center, used to run the kayak program for Outward Bound in Costa Rica, and was a registered EMT.

So, why was he calling *me*?

Turns out he had gotten crossways with his five-man team after this year's preliminary race and had re-registered to do the race solo. But he wasn't very fired up about going solo, plus he was inspired that I was racing for charity.

He shared his details, and I shared my infinitely less impressive Safari-related training stats. Finally I cut to the chase, "Phil, what I lack in experience and physical power, I will make up for in mental strength. I am a machine. I am fun. I have drive. And I absolutely WILL NOT QUIT. I will be a great partner, what will it take?"

"Well, first off, let's see if we can paddle in a boat together and keep it upright. What are you doing tomorrow?"

*Hmmm, let's see. Well, tomorrow…Tuesday…I was originally slated to be paddling in a 260-mile canoe race…but, let me check my calendar…yep, I'm free!*

Phil and I agreed to meet at the Texas Rowing Center at 8 a.m.

I had a good feeling about this. Hope rushed back like an incoming tide. I was so determined to stay in this race that I didn't even consider how crazy it was that I might be paddling across half of Texas with a complete stranger.

The phone calls kept pouring in throughout the evening. A guy from South Padre Island, a professional sand castle artist, was on the forum looking for a partner. A man named CJ who runs the safety boat in the bay stretch of the race called to say he'd paddle with me. He hadn't done the Water Safari in about seven years but he felt bad for me and generously offered to do it. Another guy called who wanted to race tandem aluminum, which was my original category. He had a previous Safari finish but hadn't registered this year because of an injury. He was eager to paddle in the Safari again and took the race delay as a sign that he should get back in it.

I was gracious and honest with everyone. But Phil was the first viable candidate who reached out, so I was focused on trying to make that work. Everyone who knew Phil raved about his paddling skills and agreed we'd make a good team.

I went to bed with my mind racing and a feeling of cautious optimism. *Please Lord, keep me in that boat tomorrow and don't let me make an absolute fool of myself!*

# CHAPTER 6

# RIVERBANK HANDSHAKE

*"The first time someone shows you who they are, believe them."*
–MAYA ANGELOU

On Tuesday morning, June 15th, I met Phil at the Texas Rowing Center on the edge of Lady Bird Lake, which is the section of the Colorado River that flows through downtown Austin. Often referred to as "The Treadmill," Austin Safari paddlers train many hours on this stretch of calm water when they don't have time to get down to the race course. But we needed a test run on the real deal so we made the drive down to San Marcos.

Phil Meyer was in his early forties, never married, and had no kids. Originally from New York, he still had the accent although he had lived all over the world. He was a passionate competitive paddler, a natural athlete, and an engineer by trade.

Phil wasn't interested in racing in my 17' aluminum canoe, which Banning and I had affectionately named "The Beast." It wasn't sleek or sexy, it wasn't built for speed, and it was super heavy to carry in the portages. What it lacked in athleticism, though, it made up for in durability. It would bounce off stumps and rocks in the river, and we could drag it on grass and light gravel without damaging the hull.

It was a forgiving and protective ride for a couple of Safari novices.

Not long after Banning and I committed to racing for charity, we were mulling over ideas for an official team name that might blend our love of fishing with our newfound interest in paddling. In a brilliant twist of wordsmithery and, frankly, a grasp at the obvious, it came to us in a flash: Team Paddlefish.

It seemed only fitting that we were aligning ourselves with a slow, lumbering fish with the loveable underdog appeal of Eeyore or Snuffleupagus. A homegrown, bottom-dwelling American creature that sucks up zooplankton and turns it into prized caviar; diamonds from coal, if you will. From there we added the tagline "Ain't Nothin' Pretty About It" and slathered it all over our website, social media sites, t-shirts, hats and stickers.

We were world famous. Locally.

Phil was more accustomed to the sleek, custom Safari-style boats, which looked more like sculling shells than canoes. At this point I didn't care how I got down that river, as long as I got down that river. While I didn't shed a tear over parting ways with The Beast, I was secretly hoping that if Phil took me on as a partner, he would also agree to adopting the Team Paddlefish name.

Phil had already located a Safari boat that we could rent for the race, and was confident we could doctor it up in time (as long as I could stay in it). Our plan was to pick it up from one of his friends in San Marcos and take it out for a test run.

The "Double Trouble" was 24-feet long and made of black composite material. It was considerably lighter than The Beast, and that was appealing for portages, but it was also more delicate so we had to be careful around stumps and rocks. The length made it faster, but more technical to steer. It was very narrow, just about the width of my hips, again making it faster, but very tippy compared to what I had trained in for the past year. The seats were set lower to the hull, which offered more stability, but also more stress on our hips.

Unfortunately, the new $290 paddle I just purchased, custom fit for the aluminum canoe, would now have to be shortened since the new boat placed me much closer to the waterline.

Phil and I took the boat out on a relatively placid section of the San Marcos River and paddled for a few leisurely miles. When I first got in the boat I felt like an elephant on a tightrope, *whoa, whoa, loose hips, deep breath, settle in.* Whenever I felt shaky, a deep calm breath seemed to settle me into the boat and melt away the wobbles. Immediately I could feel that my core muscles were the key to keeping myself upright.

There's that word again.

When I first started learning how to paddle and train, everyone that helped me sang the same chorus, "It's all about the core. Use your core. Paddle from your big muscles in the center. Rotate from your abdomen. It's all about the core."

I've never liked abdominal work and prefer not to expend energy on that region—physical or mental. I like to wear breezy hippy tops and pretend that whole area doesn't exist. Un-tucked and belt-free is how I roll. It's just not my best asset. Before this race, my version of "working on my core" meant using expensive eye cream on my stomach. And, unfortunately, I can tell you straight up that untold gallons of cocoa butter and fancy Vitamin E lotions haven't erased the pregnancy stretch marks, which fan out across my lower abdomen like flames on the hood of a Trans Am.

I just don't like thinking about my stomach. Also, "core" is just a phonetically unattractive word. Core. Nothing good even rhymes with it. Bore, chore, snore, spore, war, whore.

But as I tried to do throughout the process of training for this race, I respected those who took the time to mentor me and remained open to their suggestions. And of course they were right. Core was king, or in my case queen. The stronger my abs became, the stronger paddler I became. I had more power in the portages.

My back felt protected. Abdominals were like the boiler room of this ship, providing all the power and fuel behind the scenes. They lived layers below deck, in the shadow of the all-glorious shoulders, which were stretched, rubbed and unfurled before each training run like decorated sails.

Miraculously I managed to get through our inaugural paddle run without tipping us over and dunking Phil. This boat had a rudder controlled with foot pedals by the person in the stern. I took my hand at steering and got the hang of it fairly quickly, of course this was a calm stretch of water without many turns or obstacles.

When we finished our paddle on the San Marcos and pulled the boat out of the water, Phil extended his hand and asked me to be his Safari partner. I was ecstatic. I was racing again! The past five days had been an absolute nightmare, but now I was back on track. Nothing from the last year would be wasted. I couldn't wait to get home and call Tom, my family, and my friends. My whole personal network was abuzz, rooting for me to seal the deal with Phil. Even my new Rett Syndrome community had rallied to see how they could help me find a new partner. Wasn't I supposed to be helping *them*? Their outpouring of support was humbling and inspiring.

On the way back to Austin, Phil and I discussed logistics. He was cool using the name Team Paddlefish since I had done my fundraising under that title, and he also suggested that his friend, Monica Harmon, would make a great team captain. She knew the race and had worked on a support team previously.

"Wonderful!" I told him that Tom and my dad would be there to help her out as needed.

So, with four weeks left to retool as Team Paddlefish v 2.0, Phil and I started working on another list. We had to patch the boat, streamline our gear, redo our first aid kits, get different sized water bottles and drinking tubes, and return all the Hammer powdered drinks I'd purchased so we could use Phil's brand, which tasted worlds better. We had to Seal-a-Meal all of our food and gear and get a custom spray skirt made for the boat. We had to re-register with race officials, redo the foam on our seats, and attach the GPS, SPOT Tracker, LED lights, and bilge pump. Beyond that there wasn't much else to do, well, besides log as many training miles as possible until race day.

As we pulled into Austin, our dialog devolved from intense logistics to more conversational topics. As we were making small talk about each other's backgrounds, Phil asked, "So how'd you get into this race in the first place?"

# CHAPTER 7

# LEARNING CURVE

*"In matters of style, swim with the current; in matters of principle, stand like a rock."*
–THOMAS JEFFERSON

In the spring of 2007, I was leaving Sportsman's Finest, our local fly shop in Austin, when I bumped into a guy named Eric Wilder, whom I hadn't seen in a couple of years. Our acquaintance was superficial at best, so I give him full credit for placing a face and recognizing me. We bantered a bit about fishing; it was fun to learn that he was so into it, and I asked if he was at the fly shop to gear up for a specific fishing trip.

"Actually, I'm getting some clothes for a canoe race that I'm training for—The Texas Water Safari," he said. "San Marcos to Seadrift. It's pretty intense and kind of hard to explain. But it's a really cool race; you should check out the website."

Over the next couple of years, more people brought up the Texas Water Safari in a string of completely unrelated conversations. Inexplicably I was curious to dig a little further and learn more about the race. Perhaps it was because of the randomness, or the sheer number of times I heard the race mentioned in chance, unconnected settings.

There are no coincidences.

In April of 2009, I woke up early one morning, unable to sleep, and took to the internet for some surfing. Curious about the random mentions of this canoe race, I did a Google search and found the Texas Water Safari website.

*Yikes, 260 miles? Why on God's green earth would someone want to spend so much time on the water unless fishing was involved?*

I continued scrolling and reading and then I clicked on their photo gallery. There were shots of people covered in mud and napping in the fetal position on the riverbanks. Others were blistered from the sun and pouring dirty river water over their heads and down their shirts. There were shots of canoes tipping nose-first over concrete dams with gear and paddlers splattering all over the place.

*Good Lord, those people look absolutely miserable...*

I pressed on to Wikipedia where the accounts were infinitely more harrowing. Who would do this? I had to find out more about this race. I had to find Eric Wilder. He's the only person I knew who had done it. Eric used to work as a doorman at the Four Seasons hotel on Town Lake. I joined the health club at the Four Seasons when I was a marketing consultant in the office building next door, but kept the membership long after I left since it included access to the pool for me, Sophie and her friends. We would see Eric off and on at the hotel and he would update us periodically on his race training.

*Maybe someone at the Four Seasons would know how to reach him?*

I called and they passed me around to a few different people. They confirmed that Eric no longer worked there, but ultimately I found someone that was good friends with him, and he agreed to contact Eric and give him my phone number. Surprisingly, Eric rang me back right away, and I pressed him hard about the race.

He had finished the Water Safari twice, and despite the lingering drought we were experiencing in Central Texas, he was considering racing again in 2009. He was passionate about the race, was exceedingly generous with information and strongly encouraged me to consider racing in the Safari. His love for this event was contagious.

After hanging up with Eric, I went back to the internet and continued reading about the race. Could I do something like this? Yes, I could *totally* do this. But why *would* I do something like this?

For the next couple of days I gnawed on the idea like a leather strap clenched between my teeth; it tasted awful but I couldn't let go.

Was this the next chapter in my life, the next obstacle to conquer? Me in a four-day canoe race with mosquitoes and alligators and snakes? Did I really need to conquer another obstacle?

If I squint my eyes and concentrate real hard, I can hearken back to a time when I was a doe-eyed bride with a backdoor key to Neiman-Marcus.

Where did I get the money to shop so much back then? Because believe me, when I was in my twenties I *shopped*—it was a scheduled weekend activity. Oh, I shopped, and I hosted baby showers and supper clubs and served trendy canapés on silver trays and spent hours decorating a table with the prefect flower arrangements. All of my serving pieces and vases and picture frames still had those little numbered stickers on them, numbers that matched up with a name in a white satin wedding logbook that indicated who sent that particular gift.

Don't get me wrong, I wasn't *all* bows and frills back in the day, and this Paddlefish way of life hasn't exactly been a 180-degree transformation. I've always had a penchant for the outdoors, obviously by virtue of my parents. Hunting was their primary passion in those years, so as an only child I was their tote-along Pet Rock on all expeditions. Eventually, though, the college life scooped me up in full force and I didn't really notice during those years at UNC that my parents were spending more and more time fly fishing, and less time hunting.

Looking back, this was the era when they turned into full-fledged fishing nutcases. Their only child was gone and they fancied about the globe chasing trout and tarpon and bonefish. But I couldn't join in, much less pay attention to their activities, because I was busy flirting with fraternity boys, convincing the cutest new freshman girls to become Tri-delts, and basking in the glory of a Tarheel national championship in basketball.

Alas, college did end, and in the blink of an eye I had a fancy entry-level corporate job in Dallas, a well-decorated life, and a shiny new marriage. At this point my parents were complete trout nuts and all of our family vacations happened on rivers, which pleased my then-husband to no end. And I was totally game—how could I not be? Beautiful mountains, catching fish, relaxed people. Over time I started to get a feel for fly casting, matching hatches, and reading water. Eventually my parents built a house in Montana near the Missouri River and without knowing it I had found my home away from home.

But as much as I loved Montana, over the next few years the various pulse points of life kept me away. Sophie arrived; my career flourished; my marriage did not. Family trips continued to Montana, whenever possible, but the first time I went back there to fish after my divorce, I realized that I actually knew next to nothing about trout fishing on my own. Knots? 5x what? A guide day costs $425!

I never set out to get good at fly fishing (which is convenient, because I'm not). I just wanted to be on the water. The learning curve was steep, but over time I met each obstacle head-on and expanded my skills. When I realized that no one would be there to attach flies to tippets, I learned the improved clinch knot, and presto, I could change my fly as often as I needed. That worked fine, until the day I found a snobby pod of rising trout that refused every fly in my box. In the process, I trimmed my leader down to the point that its diameter was too large for even my biggest meat flies.

*Hmm, here's a new problem.*

There was an obvious need there that I couldn't overcome, so rod in hand I tromped out of the river in my waders, marched into a nearby fly shop, and explained my predicament. Thankfully I was friends with the guys in the shop, and they were kind enough to teach me the surgeon's knot and rebuilt my leader on the spot. Of course I was dripping wet in my waders with no means to pay for the spool of tippet, so that's the fateful day that I established my dad's first account in a Montana fly shop.

Around 2004, my love for fishing truly caught fire, but actual time on the water was becoming a problem. My pressure cooker consulting job was sucking the lifeblood out of my soul and limiting my time to fish. I couldn't seem to get into a groove on the river without a client crisis beeping in. In September of 2005, I was on my way home to Austin after a long weekend fishing on the Missouri River. After checking my bags at the airport in Helena, I begrudgingly fired up my cell phone and found seven panicky, screechy voicemails about inane client bullshit.

I totally snapped. I was done.

I boarded that plane, flew back to Austin and resigned the next morning. I alerted my ex-husband that I'd had a Norma Rae moment, so he offered to keep Sophie a few days longer while I caught my breath. I found a thrifty Southwest flight to Boise (the only flight I could afford on short notice that would take me anyplace in the West) and forty-eight hours later I was standing in the Little Wood River in Idaho. Trout fishing. I had spent all those early years looking for fish before I finally realized that I was the one at the end of the line.

Unfortunately, I had created a new problem by solving an old one. Being jobless gave me more time to fish, but no money to do it.

Sophie and I spent most of the summer of 2006 in Montana with my parents. I couldn't afford guide days anymore, and I couldn't cover much water without a boat, so I took advantage of the fact that fly fishers, by nature, are a gregarious bunch. I started loitering in the parking lots of fly shops with my hand in the air crying, "Single!" like it was a ski lift line. I would jump in the boat with pretty much anyone who wanted to fish. I'd bring the beer, snacks, whatever; I just needed a way to float.

I was getting to fish, and making all sorts of new friends, but soon it became apparent that my plan was flawed. Unfortunately, a few too many of my new fishing buddies would awkwardly try to kiss me, often in unexpected public displays at the boat ramp which would embarrass me to no end and provide endless fodder for the gossip mill in the small fishing town of Craig, Montana. I needed a new plan.

So I finagled my way into a drift boat.

The rowing part turned out to be easy, especially on a slow and forgiving river like the Missouri. My problem involved the actual act of getting my boat from land to water.

I couldn't back a trailer.

Several people tried to teach me, but those boat ramp lessons always ended in complete frustration for both parties involved. So, just as I did when I needed help with knots and tippets, I walked into a local fly shop and charmed my way around the problem. We worked a deal where they would charge a little extra for my shuttle fees for helping me with my put-ins and take-outs. People mocked me but I had no pride in the matter. I had to learn how to navigate that boat down the river so I could cover some water and catch some fish. I wasn't sure how, but I'd learn to handle a trailer later.

In the summer of 2008, the rivers of Montana served as the backdrop for my new and developing romance with Tom. We fished and flirted all over Big Sky country and Tom eventually sealed the deal when he did something infinitely more fateful and romantic than slipping a glass slipper on my foot. He taught me to back a trailer.

Clearly, it was true love.

About the same time I was researching the Texas Water Safari, and obsessing over the notion of participating in it, I boarded a plane for a girl's trip to Montana with eight ladies from Alabama that now lovingly and collectively bear the nickname, The Chicks.

It was late May of 2009, and for six days, The Chicks fished and hiked and cooked and laughed, and shook their tailfeathers on the back deck of the ranch house with no other audience but the moon, the stars, and some cows. As is often the case, fishing became a backdrop for the real stories that unfolded on this incredible vacation. I can't think of a time in my adult life where I have bonded so quickly and so deeply with a group of women. Each person brought unique talents and vibrancy to the trip. Now, I do love being a mom, but let's face it, there is nothing quite like a good old-fashioned girls' trip.

I don't recall if it was the second or third day, but I know it was fairly early in our experience together when I heard someone reference Rett Syndrome. One of the girls on the trip, Anna Luce from Mobile, had a daughter, Rancey, that had this disease.

*Rett Syndrome? Hold on...I've heard of that!*

Right before this girl's trip, a man named Bill Farnum had emailed me via my blog, *Fly Fish Chick,* and introduced himself. He explained that his daughter, Ella, suffered from a disease called Rett Syndrome and wanted to know if I would compete in his Casting 4 A Cure fundraiser. Unfortunately a scheduling conflict prevented my participation but I promised to think of a way to use my blog to get the word out.

And now here I was in this kitchen in Montana, with my new friend Anna, whose daughter Rancey also suffers from this extremely rare disease. What are the odds?

There are no coincidences.

Anna then explained Rett Syndrome to me in aching detail. The disease affects mostly little girls and is caused by a mutation in the X chromosome. It affects areas of the brain that are responsible for learning, speech, sensory sensations, mood, movement, breathing, cardiac function, and even chewing, swallowing, and digestion. Her daughter, Rancey, who was about to celebrate her nineteenth birthday, lives in a special home as her condition requires specific round-the-clock care.

When Rancey was diagnosed, Anna told her husband she wouldn't quit searching for answers until they heard their daughter speak to them.

On the airplane on the way home from Montana, it occurred to me that perhaps Rancey *is* speaking. Maybe she's speaking through Anna—or maybe through little Ella Farnum and the fly-fishing fundraisers that her dad created. Suddenly it became clear that both Rancey and Ella were, indeed, speaking to me.

I thought about my sweet Sophie. I couldn't imagine how difficult it would be if she suffered from something like this. I wasn't sure how or when but I felt compelled to do something. Rett Syndrome is virtually unknown to those who aren't directly affected; most people have never even heard of it.

Before I landed in Austin, I flipped down my tray table and scribbled some notes. I had a blog, an established audience, and a pretty loud voice. Maybe I could speak for Rancey and Ella? Maybe this was something I should get involved in? Suddenly it seemed like Rett Syndrome and I were a perfect duo. I just needed to figure out how and what I was going to do.

About a week and a half after I returned home from the Montana girl's trip, Banning and I drove down to Aquarena Springs in San Marcos to watch the start of the 2009 Water Safari. As we wove among the boats in the field next to the river I began to notice that a few teams were racing for various charities. That's when it hit me.

I could do this race to raise money for Rett Syndrome! I could do this race for Rancey and Ella.

I announced my idea to Banning, and he was on board immediately. We shook on it to make it official, and Team Paddlefish was born.

# CHAPTER 8

# LADY IN WAITING

*"Out of the frying pan of life into the fire of purgatory."*
–JAMES JOYCE

After my first paddle with Phil on June 15th, I settled into a routine of training and preparation…wait…scratch that. I settled into a routine of *re-training* and *re-preparation*.

Looking back, I'll have to say that the four weeks between the original race date and the make-up date may have been the strangest month of my life. In addition to the chaos of the flood and the race postponement, most of my friends were off traveling with their families during those weeks. Sophie trotted off to summer camp. My parents, Tom, and all of my girlfriends were in Montana, and I was spending every waking hour with a man whom I had only recently met.

I couldn't complain because I was lucky to have found a new race partner, and my family and friends had spent a pile of money to re-book flights and vacations around the revised schedule. My aunt and uncle, my cousins, Tom's nephew, my girl's fishing trip—so many people were affected by my race delay, yet they were still incredibly supportive.

But I was lonely in Austin. My phone was quiet, and my house was empty—not that I was in it very often. Phil and I were pretty much together all day, every day. We paddled. We went to Home Depot to get wire and screws. We went to Loews to get batteries. We ate what seemed like endless amounts of Vietnamese food. I didn't even realize Austin had so many Vietnamese places. I didn't understand his jokes, and he never laughed at mine. For days on end we just trained and geared up, trained and geared up, trained and geared up. Everyday was Groundhog Day with Punxsutawney Phil.

All the key players in my life had been there front and center during the crisis of the race delay, and then they earned a little break—and rightfully so. But now I was ready for them to return. I couldn't wait for my entourage to charge back into town and spirit me down that river.

But there was no time to for whining and lamenting, we had much to do and I learned a ton from Phil. He approached everything with the mind of an engineer, whether it was the meticulous decision on rigging the rudder, to strategizing our best portage plan at each and every dam and rapid. He was conservative, which I liked. His rationale was sound, not to mention he had Safari experience. His biggest concern was the bay. Last year he'd spent the night in his boat on a swampy patch of cordgrass, doling out snacks to his teammates who had run low on food. He was keenly aware of how fickle that last stretch of the race could be.

I felt inadequate on many of the boat rigging chores. Phil was conscientious and included me in every step but I didn't feel like I was pulling my weight compared to the engineer/paddler who had a garage-full of drills and tools and wires and screws. Phil took the lead on doctoring up the boat and taught me as he went. I helped paint on some resin to patch a few cuts and dings in the hull, and that did make me feel more useful. I also used a paring knife to contour a spot out of the foam in my seat. Long training runs had identified a particularly irritating place that pressured my tailbone and nearly drove me mad from the pain.

Meanwhile, as we prepared with a sense of methodical urgency, Mother Nature continued to mess with my overwrought mind. We watched the news anxiously as Hurricane Alex barreled toward the Texas coast. On June 30th it made landfall in Mexico, but pushed rain up into South Texas that seemed to linger well past its welcome. Around July 8th I was a nervous wreck as a Tropical Depression threatened the already soggy and saturated Texas coast. I was partially numb, yet also terrified at the thought of another race delay. Luckily that storm lost steam and didn't produce too much extra rain. It seemed we were on track.

Our new team captain, Monica Harmon, joined us for lunch one afternoon on Phil's living room floor as we took a small break from the gearing-up process. It was a nice opportunity before the race to get to know her in the real world, a world that still involved basic social skills and hygiene. Immediately I could see that Monica was sharp, kind, upbeat and organized. Plus, she was exceedingly enthusiastic about serving as our team captain.

The final days of the final week seemed to drone on and on as we camped out at Phil's house to wrap up preparations. On one of our last training runs on the still-swollen San Marcos, I had been in the stern steering when I misjudged my line as we were flying toward a small logjam. Phil screamed, "Go right, right, right!" I corrected with a too-sharp right turn that fishtailed the stern way out to the left. When we slammed hard into a massive tree trunk in the middle of the river, I somehow managed to pummel my thigh so violently that it literally knocked the wind out of me. At that point there was another item added to the to-do list: patch the 5-inch gash that I put in the left side of the boat. Meanwhile I was especially proud of the massive resulting bruise on my left thigh that radiated an extraordinary palette of blues, purples, greens and reds. Without question my most visually dramatic Water Safari battle scar.

In the last couple of days leading up to the race, we also had to make final clothing selections, ensuring there were no seams or tags that were going to chafe. We had to nix non-essential gear and food to lighten the load. Phil was the ounce-counter and he was relentless in his load-trimming. He tossed out one of our extra battery packs. He ditched the off-the-shelf first aid kit and made his own with bare essentials. He was an EMT, so I trusted him, but I really wanted to take that vial of Benadryl anti-itch gel. It didn't make the cut. He kept trying to reduce my food supply. I resisted vehemently, but ultimately we compromised on quantities. He warned that even fiberglass patches and decorative boat stickers add up. Ounces turn to pounds in the blink of an eye.

Most importantly, we had to vacuum pack everything with a Seal-a-Meal machine, or suffer the consequences of our precious haul being soaked by funky river water: each individual portion of powdered drink mix, each individual morsel of carefully rationed food, spare sunglasses, spare hat, spare rain jackets, spare shirts.

After a lot of research and discussions with Safari veterans, I had set a goal of consuming 280 calories per hour during the race. With four days of heat, humidity, and intense physical exertion, I wasn't about to let lack of energy become a factor.

A lot of thought went in to my food list, but I finally narrowed it down to natural sports foods like Clif bars, Clif Shot Bloks, Hammer electrolyte gels, and Bobo's Organic Peanut Butter Oat bars. Several racers had advised me to eat "whatever tastes good coming back up" or "eat like you have the flu." So I also had a number of bland items like Lorna Doone cookies, baked Cheetos, and Pringles. I was told that Pringles were especially great because I wouldn't have to waste any energy chewing them. I could stick them in my mouth, enjoy the salt, and let them melt. Phil had packed a lot of beef jerky, trail mix, and small candy bars. I tried the beef jerky but it was exhausting to chew, so I ruled it out.

Sealing up our food and gear was unbearably time consuming and we literally burned through five Seal-a-Meal machines. Luckily Wal-Mart had a liberal return policy so we just kept taking them back and getting new ones.

By Thursday of race week, I was starting to see the light at the end of the tunnel. My cough was gone, and I felt organized and energized. I was excited about my new, experienced partner and our faster boat. Most of all I couldn't wait for my parents and Tom to get back into town. On Friday morning, I decided that I couldn't put off watching the weather forecast any longer. I was still nervous about another storm, but I had to know what lay ahead.

The official forecast for Saturday through Wednesday, July 10-14 called for typical summer weather in Texas. Clear and hot. No hurricanes, no floods, no locusts.

Now...*finally*...this was actually happening.

Right?

# CHAPTER 9

# Start to Rio Vista

*"If you can't get out of something, get into it."*
–Kris Kristofferson

On Friday evening, July 9th, the entire Team Paddlefish entourage met in San Marcos for our "Last Supper" and then retired early in a local motel near the river. I was ecstatic to have Tom and my parents back in town, but bummed that my mom and Sophie would miss the start of the race. She would be picking Sophie up at summer camp the next morning, and shuttling her quickly to wherever we were on the river. It was agonizing that I wouldn't be able to give Sophie a hug (no one can touch the racers or their boats) but I knew it would be an emotional boost just to lay eyes on her. By my estimation, we would probably see her somewhere around the Luling Checkpoint.

On Saturday morning, I was happier than I'd ever imagined I could be, and curiously, much less anxious than I expected. I awoke early so I could methodically tackle each step in the preparation process. I showered, one last burst of hygiene until Seadrift. I coated my hair with conditioner before weaving it into a braid, all in the hope of keeping it from becoming a mangled bird nest. I layered delicate body parts with Desitin and Vaseline in order to prevent rashes and chafing, and then donned my meticulously-selected, training-tested Safari outfit: white quick-drying tights, a long-sleeved white shirt, and a floppy hat.

When I came down to watch the start of the race the year before, I was amazed at what some people had chosen to wear for four days in the blistering Texas sun: black straw cowboy hats, tank tops, running shorts. Had they not clued in that they were about to be ants under a magnifying glass? I couldn't control everything but I decided poor clothing choices would *not* take me out of this race. My outfit screamed function over fashion, to be sure.

After breakfast, we arrived at the starting line on the San Marcos River at about 7:30 a.m.; myself, Phil, Tom, my mom and dad, and Monica. Banning arrived soon after and I was glad that he would get to see the start before leaving town. Tim Cole was also there with his filming equipment, and he had even affixed a couple of small video cameras inside our boat to capture the chaos of the upper portion of the race.

After a rollercoaster journey to get to this point, topped off by a very isolating month of training and gearing up, I was ecstatic that most of the original Team Paddlefish crew was back *en masse*. Tosh, unfortunately, was on a plane to Anchorage, but I knew he had his finger on the pulse of our SPOT Tracker website.

The field next to the river was covered with race boats and folding chairs and piles of gear. It was a beautiful morning as racers arrived and quietly tended to their boats. News crews wandered about. Race officials wove among the teams to answer questions. Team captains were dashing back and forth to their trucks to get last minute items for their paddlers. People were stretching and packing their boats, trying to carefully zip-tie everything in its designated place. The energy level picked up as more teams arrived, and honestly, it started to feel like a party. I'd been so starved for a social life for so many weeks, and I was having a ball chatting with fellow racers, hugging friends, and celebrating the fact that we were finally set to launch.

Phil was more intense. At about 8:15 he rang the bell in the schoolyard, so to speak, and announced that recess was over. It was time to get the boat in the water and warm up. I tried not to show it, but the minute we lifted that boat, something we had done hundreds of times, I cringed at how heavy it was. I'd heard about this moment and prepared for it mentally and in training. Everyone warned that the boat would never feel as heavy as it would at the starting line when you picked it up, fully loaded, for four days on the river. Good lord, they were right. Our empty hull only weighed about 40 pounds, but fully loaded we were probably north of 130.

From day one of this odyssey, I'd heard that the psychological wear and tear of carrying the boat over and around dams, rapids, and logjams was ultimately what wore racers down the most. To prepare, some people practiced hauling their packed canoe up a ladder onto their roof. Others paddled with weights or loaded water jugs in the boat. Weeks before the race I filled a suitcase with fifty pounds of books and carried it around my house every day. I took it to the kitchen when I needed a snack. I carried it into the bathroom. I hauled it to the front door when I checked the mail. Like Tom Hanks and his volleyball, Wilson, I became emotionally attached to the piece of luggage I affectionately named "Fitty" (after the rapper Fifty Cent). I would sing my bastardized white-girl versions of "In Da Club" as I hauled Fitty to the laundry closet to wash out another set of sweaty, muddy paddling clothes.

Once on the water we paddled back and forth, warming up amidst a collection of other teams. Some were novices like me, others were Safari veterans, others major contenders to win their class. We threaded our way to the back of the pack, and settled into place to wait for the gun.

To start the race, boats are lined up in rows of six. Your starting position is determined by your time in the Safari Prelim Race as well as the date they received your registration. Originally Banning and I had a respectable starting position in the middle of the pack, right next to our friends Max and Mike who were also racing novice tandem in an aluminum canoe. We'd finished the Prelim right on their heels. But because of the race delay, Phil and I had to re-register as new partners and we lost our original starting positions. We were starting at the very back and, frankly, we were fine with that. Phil explained that the adrenalin and machismo of the six-man boats up-front is something to avoid. Once they get up a full head of steam, they're not going to slow down or alter course to avoid another team that's blocking their path to glory. This four-day 260-mile race is nei-ther won nor lost in the first five minutes—unless you get caught up in the starting line frenzy and break a paddle or gash your boat. Which, I'm told, has happened.

We were perfectly content hanging back and avoiding the panic. In fact, with our boat in the water, we stood on an adjacent concrete walkway during the National Anthem, the opening prayer, and the emcee's final instructions. It would take several minutes for fifteen some-odd rows of Safari boats to get moving, so Phil and I saw no sense in placing our tailbones in those seats even one second longer than we needed to. Other than the crowds cheering from the banks, it was a rather anticlimactic start. We were the last team to start paddling, literally the furthest boat from Seadrift. We started the race in 94th place.

Our Team Paddlefish support crew cheered as we shoved off, and then they sprinted to their cars to follow us downriver. Monica had her SUV loaded with our essential support gear, and Tom and my dad each had their own rental car to assist her with ice, water, and food runs along the race route.

*The Safari had started.*

After a quarter mile of easy paddling, I had the first of many buckets of Texas Water Safari ice water thrown in my face. We had to portage a small dam that we'd never done together. This stretch of water wasn't open to paddlers except on race day. The crowds of other boats trying to figure out which way to go was rattling me as we struggled to wrestle the boat down an awkward seam in the middle of an island with rocks and tree roots. Our once fast and agile boat was now behaving like an obese toddler being dragged out of a Chuck E. Cheese with his heels dug in. People were crowding around us and trying to squeeze through. Teams were screaming at each other. Phil was shouting instructions at me but I couldn't really understand what he wanted me to do.

*Okay, so NOW the Safari had started.*

The first seventeen miles of this race are nothing but bumper car combat paddling. In many places the banks are high and crumbly with overhanging foliage. Tree stumps and branches lean over the river, and the flow is constantly divided by rocks, light rapids, old bits of mill structure, and dams. The hairpin turns are tough to navigate even when you're the only 24-foot boat on the river; but on race day, with dozens of boats still mostly clumped together, you have to make it through tight narrow turns with two or three other boats pushing through at the same time.

Adding to the confusion of a large number of boats on a narrow, winding river was the fact that the Safari is a huge spectator event. While the throngs of shouting and cheering bankside revelers were heart-warming, the hordes of swimmers and tubers blocking chutes and rapids were extremely annoying.

The whole maniacal brew of activity and noise had me flustered. I tried to put on blinders, sit up straight and paddle the way I'd been trained, but I felt like I was living inside a video game with loud noises and flashing lights, obstacles to dart around and jump over, and raging firebombs and swooping pterodactyls to avoid. It was an auditory and visual assault on the senses.

After less than a mile we reached Rio Vista Dam, a popular set of rapids where spectators gather in huge numbers. Last summer, during my first visual introduction to the Texas Water Safari, Banning and I gathered here to watch the paddlers rush through. The original Rio Vista Dam once stretched across the entire river, but age, erosion and manmade intervention opened a chute in the middle of the structure. The dam is only about four feet tall, no big deal at all to portage, but some teams choose to run the chute instead of playing it safe and hauling their boats out for a quick portage. On race day, last summer, we watched in dumbfounded amazement as boat after boat tried to run the chute with very poor results. Some made it through unscathed, but we watched at least a dozen teams tump and loose half of their meticulously arranged gear only minutes into the race.

With 94 boats still clumped together so near the start of the race, Team Paddlefish strategically opted not to run the chute at Rio Vista. Why risk breaking the boat, or a morale-crushing tump so early in the race?

When Phil and I reached the dam we pulled off on river left and lifted the boat out of the water. Crowds were screaming and our support team was pushing ahead of us to clear a portage path through the mob of bankside spectators. When we reached the spot that we had scouted for re-launch, I was feeling really good about our decision to portage and I was relieved that the first significant Safari obstacle was behind us. But then, as we lifted the boat up and over a low concrete wall to re-enter the river, my worst case scenario happened.

On a seemingly benign physical maneuver that I had performed hundreds of times over the past year, a surgically-repaired disk in my lower spine decided to revolt.

# CHAPTER 10

# Rio Vista to Cottonseed Rapid

*"Even if you're on the right track, you'll get run over
if you just sit there."*
–Will Rogers

In 2002, I was walking through a strip mall parking lot in Nashville, holding a two-year-old Sophie, when we were hit by a crazy old bat driving her sensible sedan insensibly fast. She never even saw us. Luckily Sophie was unscathed, but my lower back was a wreck.

Three weeks later I was traveling on a train and when I reached to pull a suitcase off the luggage rack, my lower spine, which had been inflamed since the car impact, gave out completely. I was incapacitated in New York City for five days with two herniated discs.

I refused to have surgery.

In 2004 I was taking my roller bag down from the overhead bin on an airplane and re-herniated one of the disks that had moderately healed itself. At that point my doctor demanded surgery.

When I decided to do the Texas Water Safari in 2009, my back was my biggest concern. I immediately started doing Pilates to strengthen my abdominal and back muscles, and I researched the pros and cons of wearing back braces in the race. I ultimately decided against one because several racers advised that a brace would allow for lazy posture while paddling, thus making the situation worse.

In July of 2009, just one year before the race, I was in Montana with Tom and his nephews. After fishing, one day, I was helping load the drift boat on the trailer and, snap! With one awkward twist I wrenched my back—again—and undid my surgeon's expensive handiwork.

With the help of a seemingly endless supply of Motrin and a short stint with Prednisone (my pharmacist calls it The Devil's Drug; my boyfriend would have to agree) my back survived the summer, and by September I was able to start paddling. Over the past year of training there were a couple more lower back twinges, but none serious, and none since January when our intensive training began. I knew when I started the race that this was a possibility, but I had tried to block it out of my mind.

When I climbed back into the canoe at Rio Vista I was racked with pain but I tried not to show it. There was no way that I was dropping out of this race so soon, so I gritted my teeth, clenched my core and held my posture while we resumed paddling in the midst of insanity.

Tom would later tell me that he saw a solo paddler pull out of the race at this exact point. The man's wife and son were yelling at him not to do it, but he still quit at Rio Vista. Perhaps he too was injured and it was unavoidable, but I couldn't fathom turning in a DNF (Did Not Finish) only ¾ of a mile into a 260-mile race.

As we paddled away from the lunacy of Rio Vista, Phil seemed agitated with everything I was doing. At one point he barked at me, sharply, "Why did you draw stroke right, then?"

"Uh, because we were about to hit a tree stump?"

"Don't draw stroke unless I tell you to! Just paddle. You just keep the pace in the bow and let me handle the steering. You're the metronome; just keep the tempo of the stroke. Don't draw unless I tell you to draw."

*What the...? Who is THIS Phil?*

I was actually working my butt off, and I really thought we were going to hit that stump. I was pissed, and I was worried about my back. This race sucked. What had it done with my partner? I had come to know Phil as a patient teacher, a light-hearted mentor and all around good guy who was inspired to race for charity with a novice as opposed to chasing a solo title. Where was the cucumber cool partner I'd been training with for the past month? I didn't remember signing up for Operation Chastise Christine.

He must have sensed my irritation. "Listen, I'm not trying to be harsh. I'm just trying to get us through this."

"I get that, Phil, but you don't have to ask me condescending questions like that. I am actually trying my hardest." Uncharacteristically, I added, "And you're not always right."

Despite my passive-aggressive quip, I knew Phil *was* right about the bowman and the metronome reference. Every position in the boat had a role. The previous year, Phil was third seat in a five-man boat; he was the power. He didn't steer, he didn't navigate. He didn't have to memorize the river, although he knew it well.

In order to leverage my natural advantages, I had made it my mission to memorize every stretch of the river as best as I could. I had analyzed maps and Google Earth on the computer, memorized mileage between checkpoints and their cutoff times, and even visualized reaching the twelve checkpoints each time I knocked out another ten-minute segment on the rowing machine. Knowing the river route was something I could control.

Unlike his third seat position in last year's race, this year Phil was in the stern and in charge of steering, which meant he called out when I should do a draw stroke. Basically the person in the bow has to draw, or dig in with the paddle blade in order to change directions quickly, forcing the boat to make a dramatic turn that the rudder can't handle on its own. The person in the bow also sets the pace of the paddle strokes. We had to paddle in perfect sync to maximize hull speed. Since I couldn't see him, it was his job to match his paddle stroke to mine, hence the metronome comparison. It's easier to match a stroke that has a consistent tempo. In addition to steering, Phil was in charge of calling out the huts. "Hut!" meant it was time for both of us to switch and paddle on the opposite side.

Vowing not to mess up again, I refocused my efforts on paddling and tempo and left the steering up to Phil.

Minutes later we were coming around a curve heading under a bridge when Phil yelled, "Draw right! Draw right!" I could plainly see that drawing right was going to turn the bow of the boat straight into a concrete bridge piling. I had learned in training that Phil often confused right and left and I knew full well that he meant left. But I was still seething about the way he'd chastised me, so in a classic stubborn move I did precisely as I was told, which drove the nose of the boat straight into the bridge piling.

"Did you mean the other right?" I sniped sarcastically. Immature, I know, but I just couldn't restrain myself. Phil didn't seem fazed.

The next obstacle was Thompson Island Dam. It seemed like we had already been paddling for hours, but when I glanced at my watch it was only 9:30 am. With my lower back still in full revolt, we once again got out and awkwardly worked the heavy boat down a slippery concrete slope, and into a trickle of water that was flowing down to the main river. Any time we could let the water help carry the weight of boat, the better. Many racers burn themselves out on the San Marcos and little advantages add up to help conserve energy.

A half-mile downriver we had to get out again at the Thompson Island Road Bridge. This is the place that had tortured Banning and me during training, the place where the overhanging trees smacked us like a cheap piñata. Turns out, though, that Phil knew what Banning and I didn't. There was a cut at river left that bypassed the evil tumping trees. From there all we had to do was hop out on an easy bank, lift the canoe up and over a narrow spit of ground, and drop it back in the water.

For the next half-hour we had a break in the chaos of portages and obstacles. We were passing boats (morale boost) and affably chatting with a few other teams along the way. It wasn't terribly hot, yet, but we forced ourselves to drink some electrolyte mix from our drinking tubes.

At around 10 a.m. we hit the Blanco River confluence. It's a fairly unremarkable spot, but for some reason I always liked reaching it during training. It was a rare chance to catch our breath on the Upper San Marcos, and for some reason it felt like progress. A whole other river was jumping on the bandwagon, getting on board like a new recruit in a pyramid scheme.

After another river mile we reached Cummings Dam, the first sizable structure we would have to portage. Constructed in 1914, it was designed to push water back up into the mouth of the Blanco River that could be drawn out for irrigation. The dam was also used for generating electricity. The water drops over the dam vertically into a deep pool that's littered with mangled concrete and rebar. Unrelated to the Safari, a few people have actually drowned here after getting pulled over the dam and trapped in the debris below. It's a tangled and dangerous mess where rescuers have actually lost their grappling hooks while trying to drag for submerged bodies.

The scene when we arrived at Cummings was absolute freaking pandemonium. This portage was hairy enough without throngs of adrenaline-crazed racers shouting and muscling their way through. The water typically rages over Cummings Dam, which stands roughly twelve feet high. On the downriver side of the dam, near the right bank, there is a crude wooden ladder that's bolted flush against one of the concrete buttresses that angles down to the riverbed.

We had done this before, but this time it didn't go so well. After stopping the boat in a stagnant pool on the right, above the dam, we hoisted it atop the concrete wall near the ladder and then spun the boat 90-degrees. With the boat teetering like a seesaw on the ledge, I clambered around to the right and down the bank to the foot of the dam while Phil held the boat in place up above. My job was to guide the bow of the boat from below while Phil eased it down the ladder with the stern rope. Unfortunately, with all of the extra cargo, the bow of the boat was buried in the gravel and I was struggling to move it an inch at a time.

Phil was screaming, "Come on! Let's go! Move it!" People were behind him up there, anxious to get their turn on the ladder. He must have felt them breathing down his neck and was transferring the tension down to me. It was painful and stressful but we finally got the boat down the ladder and back in the water. I couldn't wait for the pack to thin out in this crazy race. I could tell Phil was anxious around other racers when we were in these clutch moments.

We pressed on.

Despite a team that bailed out of their boat right in front us heading into Old Mill Rapids (the equivalent of stopping your car in the middle of an on-ramp during screaming rush hour traffic), we handled the rapids at the old broken down mill fairly well. We flew past them on the right through the first stretch of fast water and then we bailed out of the boat to swim it through the center rapid and the old window-like remnant of the original dam. It also felt nice to cool off in the water and have a chance to pee.

With barely enough time to catch our breath, we quickly arrived at Broken Bone Rapids. This spot had not been kind to Banning and me, nor to Phil and me. We had all tumped there during training. Basically the river curves to the left, so centrifugal force pulls the boat wide to the right and into a nasty wave train. Our plan was to hug the left and paddle as hard as we could. We came hot into the turn and managed to stay left longer than usual. We took on water, which forced us to pull over and empty the canoe, but technically we didn't tump. A moral victory that I happily accepted.

On deck was Cottonseed Rapids which were created by the remnants of another old dam. Only nine miles into the race route, Cottonseed was one of the most aggressive rapids on the course. Wipeouts and collisions happened with frequency, thus it was a popular spot for crowds to assemble and gawk. In the high-sided aluminum canoe, Banning and I had always run Cottonseed without a problem. Given our lower profile and more delicate boat, not to mention our lack of training together on those rapids, Phil suggested that we portage part of Cottonseed. I was okay with that.

The compromise was a semi-portage that we had polished in training. Basically we paddled into the rapids and took the first right turn and set of waves. This involved paddling with all of our might, Phil steering like a madman, and me doing a draw stroke to avoid some boulders and then leading us into the softer water at river right.

It worked, but it wasn't exactly as smooth as we'd done it in training. The chaos of the spectator scene was insane. Someone was ringing a cowbell. Spectators were cheering. People were shouting and waving to get our attention, and there were race officials standing in the middle of the river, ostensibly to signify perilous obstacles.

It completely threw me.

Phil was barking at me about my draw stroke, even after safely reaching the portage spot. From there we had to crawl the boat over and around a big pile of rocks, then jump back in and paddle like crazy to avoid another tumping spot that had tripped us up during training. It was a large rock dividing the main flow, and against our instinct, we had to paddle hard and straight for it to avoid a back eddy, then cut right at the last second just before hitting the rock.

Tom didn't know that we knew about the rock, and he was standing on the bank at the bottom of Cottonseed warning us about its location. "There's a rock right there! Right there!" he yelled.

Sarcastically, Phil uttered, "We got it *Tom*."

My face went flush with rage. Good heavens, Tom was try-ing to help us! Just a week or so before, we had actually bailed out to avoid the *same* rock because *we* hadn't seen it in time. His criticism of everyone around us—competitors and teammates—was really start-ing to wear on me.

Despite the tension and chaos, we did survive Cottonseed Rapids. It wasn't a textbook run by any standard, but we were on the other side at 11 a.m. with the boat intact, and only 251 miles left to paddle.

# CHAPTER 11

# Cottonseed Rapid to Staples

*"It is not the mountain we conquer but ourselves."*
–Edmund Hillary

About two miles downriver from Cottonseed, we reached the idyllic town of Martindale, best known as the setting for the remake of *The Texas Chainsaw Massacre*.

This spot has two obstacles: Martindale Dam and the Martindale low water crossing. They're close together so it's a tough call whether you should portage the dam, get back in the boat to paddle, and then portage the crossing. We decided to knock out both in one fell swoop. The total portage distance was about 220 yards.

We pulled over at river right, just above the dam, and easily slid the boat onto the flat bank. It was a nice grassy stretch with few rocks, so we could safely drag the boat without damaging the hull. Dragging was easier than carrying, but I was still worried about my back. We both took a grip on the bow, lifted it up, and dragged the stern up the grassy slope and around the bushes about twenty feet away from the water's edge. The boat felt heavy, so *damn* heavy, and the sun was starting to wear on me. It was about 11:30 a.m. and pushing 90 degrees. I tried to make sure to use my thighs and hold perfect posture, terrified that I was worsening my back without knowing it. We trudged ahead, frequently switching places to alternate arms. After an uphill stretch we had to drag that obese and vile lug of a boat through a metal fence, carry it over a gravel road, then back downhill to the river. In training I handled this portage with no problem, laughing and talking all the way. But for some reason today it really kicked me in the teeth.

A crazed lunatic in a leather mask and wielding a chainsaw would have been a welcome relief at this point.

Next up after Martindale was Tekins Rapids. Again, for Banning and me in our high-sided aluminum canoe, Tekins had never been a problem, but Phil and I tumped here every time during training. In order to stay upright we needed to paddle fast and hard to keep up our speed. But Phil said when things got turbulent I either paused my paddling or touched the side of the boat as we were going over...thus *ensuring* that we would go over.

When I realized that Tekins was coming up, I resolved to paddle like a demon and keep us upright. We came upon the signature tree in the middle of the river and then three options: a seam of water curving far left where we couldn't see potential obstacles; the middle route that was shallow and rocky and requiring another mini-portage (dragging); and the far right seam where we had tumped numerous times. Neither of us wanted to portage again. It was incredibly draining getting in and out of the boat and moving the dead weight of the canoe, so we took the far right seam and paddled like crazy.

We tumped. At least we were consistent.

On the upside, Phil couldn't determine one thing that I'd done wrong this time. Another moral victory.

We floated and swam the boat down to a spot where the water came just above my knees. At that depth we could flip the boat over and bail the water that had accumulated in our spill. I was still beat down from the Martindale portage and had trouble lifting the boat high enough to dump the water out. I could tell I was frustrating Phil, hell I was frustrating myself. I tried again and again to get the boat high enough to dump water out without scooping more in. It took a few attempts for me to lift it up with my thighs and arms, but finally I got it above water level and we were able to drain it completely.

The last three miles to the Staples Checkpoint were dead water and slow going. We could tell we were getting close to another major dam when the river turned into suck water. I don't remember any laughing or conversation during this stretch. The obstacles subsided but the signature Team Paddlefish jocularity was still not there. Suddenly I had too much time to worry about my back. What if I had herniated another disk? In my previous back trouble episodes it wasn't until the next day that the severity of the consequences set in. By that point I was usually completely immobile and racked with searing spasms up my spine and down my legs. I couldn't stomach the thought of that happening during this race, so I decided to concentrate on the things I could control.

First, I bit down on the mouthpiece of my drinking tube and spit out the first sip to make sure I didn't ingest any river gunk. During portages the tubes would flail around in the bottom of the boat where river water could seep into the bite piece. Drinking river water was a surefire way of contracting Giardia. Banning said that the bacteria came from animal urine in the water. I had no idea if that part was true, but I was dead set on avoiding a gastric meltdown, whether its origin was swamp folklore or medical fact.

After taking a long pull from my water jug, I tore into another food pack. Normally I couldn't stand the monotony of this flaccid water above Staples, but after the insanity of the race so far, I was glad to have a free moment to regroup and make some deals with God about my back. Truthfully, the prayer was less about the actual health of my back and more about my pride and finishing the race.

Phil and I weren't chatting much, so I heard the din of the Staples Checkpoint crowd well before I saw it. I couldn't wait to see Tom and my dad and the whole team.

The Staples Dam is another big one with a few portage options. Some teams were going down the left side, which was less crowded, but pretty hairy. Banning and I had always taken the aluminum boat down a rickety metal staircase just right of the dam, but this required a deep water start on re-entry and Phil was concerned that there was too much water flow to safely pull that off so close to the base of the dam.

We opted for a long conservative portage that required a mix of carrying and dragging the canoe. We went up and around, and through the walkway of a private "Safari-friendly" home. I was shocked at the crowds of people all over the banks and the hillside. This wasn't just another dam to portage, it was the first official check-point of the race. Monica would have to sign in our time with the race officials. How would she ever find us? Phil didn't seem con-cerned because we didn't slow down to look for Monica. We pushed through the people and back toward the water as fast as we could while carrying our 130-pound dead relative.

Truthfully, the team captain was supposed to be there on alert waiting for his or her team, no matter the hour of day or night. Sometimes they would send other support team members upriver to keep a lookout and signal when the team was coming in. Monica had asked Tom and my dad to help with this, as well as scoot recreational families out of the way as we plowed into a checkpoint.

I kept my eyes on the ground and powered through the gru-eling portage, trying to keep pace with Phil. I would soon learn that he did not like the social scene of the checkpoints and wanted to spend as little time as possible at each one of them. I was hoping for a brief exchange with our support team. That wouldn't happen.

Somehow they found us among the masses on the backslope down below the dam. It looked like pit stop row at a NASCAR event.

We tossed our empty water jugs and drinking tubes on the ground along with what little trash we had accumulated. Per the rules, Tom and my dad passed fresh water jugs to Monica and she handed them to us to wedge into our foam placeholders. Along with the water refills, she handed us each a tube sock filled with ice and sealed with zip ties. This was an age-old Safari trick. The ice sock is wrapped around the neck to keep the carotid artery cool, which in turn cools the body. Tom and my dad watched as I stuffed a second ice sock into the elastic of my shorts, placing it on my lower back. It was so cold against my overheated flesh that it almost felt like dry ice on bare skin.

"I tweaked my back at Rio Vista." I'm guessing they were alarmed by this bit of news but I couldn't really make eye contact and absorb their concern that moment.

Banning was there rooting for us. He was scheduled to fly out the next day, but at least he got to see us through the first checkpoint. Tim Cole was filming. My dad and Tom were upbeat and helpful, and Monica was pleasant, cool, and encouraging while she managed the exchange of water and logged us in with the race officials. They were all just as excited as they were when we'd left them at the start. But I was miserable. I had nothing to say; I barely made eye contact.

We left the checkpoint sooner than I preferred, but it was nice to leave the crowds and the nuttiness. Other boats were getting back into the river, which made me feel like we were wasting time. Phil was all business and very intense.

As we paddled off, I could hear clapping and people shouting, "Go Team Paddlefish! Way to go Phil and Christine!" I appreciated their cheers but I felt guilty because I didn't have the gusto to match their positive attitude. I had no mojo, no fight in me. I had actually made it to my first checkpoint in the Texas Water Safari with plenty of time to spare, but there was no celebratory tone, no team spirit. I was numb…then again maybe it was the tube sock filled with ice that I'd stuffed down my pants.

## Staples Checkpoint

| | |
|---|---|
| CUTOFF TIME: | SATURDAY 3:00 P.M. |
| OUR TIME: | SATURDAY 12:53 P.M. |
| PLACE: | 66TH |
| TIME ELAPSED: | 3 HOURS AND 53 MINUTES |
| MILES PADDLED: | 17 |
| MILES TO GO: | 243 |

# CHAPTER 12

# Staples to Luling

*"How could drops of water know themselves to be a river?*
*Yet the river flows on."*
–Antoine de Saint-Exupery

Just after Staples we immediately ran into another obstruction. It looked like the remnants of an old road bridge, but we weren't sure. All that remained were a row of square wooden pilings, spaced several feet apart, and stretching across the river like some medieval torture device, or the great wooden teeth of a giant river monster.

We probably could have run straight through them, but again, trying to be conservative we eased over to a gravel bar and got out of the boat to assess the monster. Fortunately it didn't require a portage, so we were able line up the bow, re-board, and sprint between its teeth.

About nine miles further down, we passed the Fentress boat ramp where we often took out at the end of a training run. Passing Fentress boosted my spirits; crowds were cheering and I knew that we had a brief reprieve in the mental game of avoiding river obstacles. The trees in this area were tall and lush and the fields on the left were almost pastoral. There was a popular campground just below Fentress called Leisure Camp. I was excited to get there because I had some friends who were coming out to spend the day with their kids and to cheer for Team Paddlefish. I had given Tom instructions on how to meet up with them and was looking forward to seeing my crew.

As we neared Leisure Camp, I was once again taken aback by the crowds. There were hundreds of people swimming and picnicking and cheering for the racers. So much for seeing my friends, this was an absolute madhouse. As we charged through the throng of human pylons in the river, I looked up suddenly and my friends Benjamin, Henley and Kevin were right there standing knee deep in the current. We literally almost hit them. They were as shocked as I was and they barely managed a "Hey! Hey Christine!" as we flew past.

I smiled and nodded quickly without breaking paddling stride. We were by them in a flash, but I didn't see Tom. Turns out he arrived just minutes after we barreled through.

We had run this section down to Luling several times over the past few months and I knew it pretty well. While some people thought it was easier than the first seventeen miles, I didn't want to let down my guard. True, there were no dams to portage, but there were fast turns, logjams, and gravel bars in the middle of the river that could catch us on a tight turn.

The trick in this section was to ride the current lines. Sometimes that meant running fast and wild way out to the left or right, leveraging the fastest moving water and not catching an edge in a slower back eddy. If the boat was moving fast and either the bow or stern slid into slower water, it would grab like quicksand and spin us around. The fastest way to Seadrift was riding the fastest water to Seadrift. No sense expending energy paddling through slow water when there was a faster seam just a few feet over. Luckily I wasn't too bad at reading water from my experience fishing and rowing a drift boat. Phil was the one actually steering us onto those faster seams, but it helped that I could read the currents and know in advance where he was headed. Everything in a tandem boat works better when the partners are actually *in* tandem.

While there were no manmade portages to worry about, this stretch of river was thick with sweepers and strainers. A sweeper is a fallen tree that lies just above the surface with current rushing beneath it. It's a hazard aptly named for its propensity to sweep paddlers out of their seats as their boat rushes beneath the branches.

A strainer is a submerged pile of logs, trunks, and limbs with water flowing through it. I first found it hard to tell the difference between a strainer and a logjam, but then I deduced that a strainer is the lightweight cousin of the logjam. Submerged strainers were the real threat. If we tumped or found ourselves swimming for any reason, it was critical to get over to the bank as quickly as possible instead of riding the current down to a select spot below. That's the easiest way to avoid getting tangled up in an underwater strainer. Strainers were the main reason that Phil didn't advocate wearing a life vest in fast-moving sections; too many straps and appendages that might get snagged.

Phil also explained that we never wanted to follow a boat closely through a strainer or logjam. If the lead boats gets stuck, which had happened to us many times, the trailing boat would plow into their stern and potentially take both teams out of the race.

Last weekend, we'd had an especially wild training run in this section. Early in the day we were paddling in fast water at river left. We were whipping through low hanging tree branches with twigs and leaves smacking us in the face. In places we had to hold the shafts of our paddles in front of our eyes for protection. At one point one of those branches grabbed the lanyard of my sunglasses and ripped them off my face.

*Dammit!*

I had trained with six different pairs of sunglasses and those were the most comfortable, and of course the most expensive. Some of the previous models pinched around my ears and gave me a headache. Some got slick with sweat and would slide down my nose, which creates a problem when you don't have an unoccupied finger to push them back up. I went home that night and ordered two more pair of Kaenons and gladly paid for overnight shipping.

On that same run, last Saturday, we were plowing under a bridge with Safari veteran West Hansen right on our tail. We didn't see the guy fishing from the bridge until his hook grabbed the stern of our boat. At about the time we noticed that the boat felt sluggish, West saw the heavy line stretching across the river and had to duck beneath to avoid a monofilament clotheslining. After pulling over to cut ourselves free, it occurred to me that the least-observant-fisherman-on-the-planet apparently never even noticed that he had snagged Moby Dick.

West Hansen is a soft-spoken Safari veteran and a paddling machine of legend. He has always been happy to lend suggestions during our bankside visits or while paddling during a training run. This year West was racing tandem with Katie, a fast-rising paddling star who had won the Women's Solo class of the Missouri 340 race. This was her first time entering the Texas Water Safari and everyone was excited to see how she and West would fare.

In addition to hooks hanging from bridges and ill-tended by absent-minded buffoons, we also had to keep an eye out for orphaned treble hooks dangling in our faces as we paddled through overhanging tree branches. Having been hooked many times by small size 18 dry flies, I couldn't imagine how awful it would be to speed into a 3/0 treble hook hanging at eye level, slathered in nasty catfish bait.

As the afternoon wore on, Phil seemed to unwind a little, although I sensed that he wouldn't fully relax until we got this tender race boat off the San Marcos. Next to the bay, he was most concerned about breaking the boat in the chaos of the upper course.

While many boats were starting to spread out, we seemed

to be leapfrogging quite a bit with a six-man team of retired Marines. They had been all the talk in the weeks leading up to the race. I think a few of them had completed the Safari before, but this year they had taken two massive aluminum canoes, cut them apart, and then patched them back together in a Frankenstein-like attempt to create a gargantuan super boat. Everyone had been talking about it, and most Safari veterans couldn't believe that they would *knowingly* fabricate one of the heaviest boats in the 48-year history of the race. Few believed they would make it to Seadrift, but the big "SEMPER FI" sticker on the side of their boat seemed to mock those that lacked faith in their resolve.

They were quite a sight on the river, and what they may have lacked in paddling coordination, they made up for with strength and testosterone. We typically tried to avoid them on the turns and we also made it a point to never follow them into a tight spot for fear that they might get stuck.

Around 3:00 p.m. I was really starting to feel the blazing sun and I badly needed a pee break. I was also hungry, but I knew we were getting close to the Luling 90 Checkpoint and I decided to stem my urges for fear of losing our momentum. After the twists and terrors of the Upper San Marcos, it was nice to be finally speeding along and banking both time and mileage.

Roughly an hour later I suddenly became aware of a familiar, pungent odor wafting across the river. Ahhhh, yes…Luling, Texas! I'd recognize that dank smell of oil anywhere.

Originally founded as a railroad town in 1874, Luling quickly became a rough-and-tumble outpost for cowboys and cattle drivers and eventually earned the moniker "The Toughest Town in Texas." Things settled down in Luling in the late 1800s when the cattle drives disbanded, and for many years, agriculture, specifically cotton, was the town's only economy. In the early 1900s, a Massachusetts transplant named Edgar B. Davis came looking for oil around Luling. A spiritual man, he professed that God sent him to Texas to look for oil and spare the hamstrung people of Luling a life as a one-crop cotton town. Having leveraged everything to drill, he was financially destitute.

On August 9th 1922 he received an insufficient funds notice from his bank because he couldn't cover a check for $7.40. That same day the well he named Rafael Rios No. I was twisting away into the Earth when it struck oil at 2,100 feet. Davis had discovered the Luling Oil Field, catapulting the small town into a completely different tax bracket. A benevolent Texas wildcatter, Davis proceeded to give generously to the residents of Luling. He never joined a church but attended all of them regularly. As Joe Jackson notes in his book *The Thief at the End of The World,* Davis regularly claimed that, "Success wasn't a matter of intelligence, or even common sense, but faith."

I had to agree with Mr. Edgar B. Davis on that point. Through the process of elimination, success in the Water Safari would have to be driven by faith because no intelligent person, nor anyone with a lick of common sense, would sign up for this.

After the smell of oil, we noticed the sound of cars, which meant we were not too far from the second checkpoint at the Highway 90 bridge. As we came around a bend, the bridge came into view, along with the checkpoint area at river left. Typically there were one or two RVs there on the weekends with people picnicking and swimming. But once again I was floored when we rounded the bend and saw the mayhem. The parking lot was packed with vehicles and people. The river was jammed with families swimming and people bobbing in inner tubes and rafts. People were perched on folding chairs on patches of gravel in the center of the river. Safari boats were struggling to find a way through.

In the midst of the madness, we saw Monica waving us down. On the high bank, trying to avoid the crowd, my mom and Sophie were also waving and yelling. Monica, Tom and my dad, were all three standing out in the water about ten or twelve feet away from the bank. We jumped out of the boat to get control and avoid plowing through a family of swimmers. Without brakes or an anchor, jumping out and hand-guiding the boat was sometimes the best way to slow things down. I had already proved that ramming into a tree was also effective, but not advised.

I had hoped we would land in waist deep water so I could pee, but it was barely knee deep. At that point, though, I was at crisis stage so I crouched down low and duck-walked next to the boat. Unfortunately, this thoroughly alarmed Tom and my dad who were still a wreck from the little bomb I'd dropped in their lap at Staples about having tweaked my back. They were shouting out, "Are you okay? Is your back okay?"

I nodded. I couldn't explain fully; things were loud and confusing.

Phil was in what I was coming to recognize as his super-serious-all-business-high-intensity checkpoint demeanor. As we moved the boat closer to them, it became harder to hold onto it. The current was strong and Monica was struggling to hold her ground. When she let go of my dad's hand to reach for our water jugs, she was nearly swept off her feet. Since Tom and my dad couldn't give us the water and ice, my dad took off his belt and wrapped it around Monica's waist, holding her secure in the current while she pulled fresh water jugs from her crate and gave us new ice socks.

It felt incredible to see Sophie after three weeks at camp, and I called up to her, "Hi Sophie! How are you? How was camp?" Heavens, she looked so tall. How long had she been gone? She looked all grown up.

"Mommy! I have a boyfriend!"

My heart leapt into my throat.

*What!?*

I couldn't process that nugget of information. I couldn't believe she was all the way up on that bank and I couldn't give her a hug. But those were the rules, and that was the extent of our reunion.

As quickly as possible we got back in the boat and paddled away from the checkpoint. I was shouting out as we picked our way through the swimmers, "Heads up! Heads Up! Coming through!" I would later learn that my friend Debbie on the Hippie Chicks team blew a whistle to get through these crowded recreational areas.

As we picked up speed there was a young boy splashing around directly in the middle of the river, right in our line. Apparently these people have no clue how difficult it is to perform evasive maneuvers in a 24-foot boat. I screamed and screamed, but he wouldn't get out of the way. His dad was standing right next to the boy but neither of them reacted. Finally, I looked directly at the dad and screamed again, "Get him out of the way! We are coming through!" I thought we were going to hit the kid. Thankfully right at the last second the dad scooped him up as we blew past them.

Frankly, it felt good to give my vocal chords a workout; they were the only body part thus far that hadn't been taxed beyond comprehension. I had been uncharacteristically quiet for most of the day. Phil had been barking orders left and right while I was focused on listening and executing. I think, too, that I was in a bit of shock at the chaos of the whole race day scene. I had been so intent on avoiding fast-moving boats and firmly-planted obstacles that I hadn't even had the time or inclination to speak.

Shouting at that kid lit a fire of confidence within me. It woke me up, it pumped me up, it goaded me back to action.

Like Samson with his hair, or Poseidon with his trident, I had my voice back.

## Luling Hwy 90 Checkpoint

| | |
|---|---|
| CUTOFF TIME: | SATURDAY 8:00 P.M. |
| OUR TIME: | SATURDAY 5:15 P.M. |
| PLACE: | 58TH |
| TIME ELAPSED: | 8 HOURS AND 15 MINUTES |
| MILES PADDLED: | 40 |
| MILES TO GO: | 220 |

# CHAPTER 13

# LULING TO ZEDLER MILL

*Evangelize – (verb) to advocate a cause with the object of making converts*
–WORLD ENGLISH DICTIONARY

Things relaxed a bit as we pulled away from the congestion of the Luling 90 Checkpoint. It helped that the next segment was a quick, uneventful six-mile cruise to Zedler Mill, the exact stretch that is also called the "Luling Paddling Trail."

Zedler Mill was built in the 1800s, mainly for milling corn and ginning cotton. Eventually a man named Fritz Zedler bought out his partners and came to own the mill outright. He made several improvements throughout the years including a sawmill, which was very productive for the community. Unfortunately, in 1888 the three-story facility burned to the ground. Luling residents rallied to help Zedler rebuild the mill, and today it is managed by the City of Luling and the Zedler Mill Foundation. It is a restored cultural center, educating visitors about the regional heritage, as well as the history of the San Marcos River.

Not long after we left the Luling 90 Checkpoint, I heard a familiar voice shouting from the right bank, "Well, hey, hey! It's Team Paddlefish!"

It was my friend Eric Wilder, his race partner, Dan Brennen plus one or two other teams taking a mid-afternoon rest in a spot of shade. I was so excited to see a familiar face, especially Eric's, and I yelled back, "Hey, how's it going? Y'all look like you're having fun!"

They invited us to join them but we were in a groove and I knew that Phil wasn't about to stop for a bankside happy hour.

I thanked them for the invite and gave them a wave with my paddle as we shuttled on past.

Phil spoke quietly behind me, "That's really frowned upon."

"What is?"

"Breaking on the banks with other teams."

"Why?"

"Because race officials don't know if food or supplies are being shared. The whole point of the Safari is you are supposed to make do with your exact provisions. Plus at night, if you are camped out together, technically you are benefiting from each other's lights, saving on battery power...hut!"

I switched my paddle to the other side. "Well, that makes sense." I liked that Phil was such a rule follower. But I also knew Eric and how much he loved this race; he wasn't going to risk a misstep. He respected the Safari way too much.

As we paddled on in silence, the shadows on the river began to lengthen and the afternoon breeze picked up. Sipping from my drinking tube, I thought back to those fun-filled summer days when Eric was working as a doorman at the Four Seasons. While I never got much out of their posh workout facilities, Sophie and I took full advantage of the swimming pool privileges.

Among all of the elegant rides waiting at the valet stand, we used to roll in looking like the Beverly Hillbillies with bird poop all over the windshield, duct tape holding my seat together, and all sorts of bags and tennis rackets and lunchboxes and half-eaten breakfast bars piled high in the passenger seat. Fishing guides who live out of their trucks have less crap in their vehicles than I do.

When the valet would open the car door, pool noodles would explode in every direction and kids would clamber out of the backseat in a swirl of blowing homework papers and Whataburger sacks. Simply stated, we weren't subtle when we showed up to swim, and it's not surprising that Eric so quickly recognized my car that day when I bumped into him in the fly shop parking lot.

Eric was my Safari Godfather from the start. He spelled it all out for me in painstaking detail: above else, you must survive the San Marcos…don't take too much ibuprofen; your body metabolizes things differently in extreme situations, and ibuprofen has been known to give people uncontrollable nosebleeds…have fun with the race…it's the coolest way to see Texas, the way the settlers and the Indians saw it…don't get too caught up in the race politics and bullshit…in the lower section you will start to lose your mind and you will argue with your partner, it's just part of it…talk to the Safari vets and listen to them, they know their stuff…rotate, rotate, rotate with each paddle stroke…paddling form is more important than power… just remember, finish your rotation with your tits to the bank…use your big muscles…don't grip too tight with your hands…don't mess with paddling gloves, if your hands can't dry they'll rot inside your gloves…don't worry about the asshole naysayers, use them to fuel you…train with your food, things you normally eat won't work in the Safari…you don't want heartburn or nausea, they'll take you down… train with extra weight, but don't take too much stuff…put extra foam on your seats, it's your throne, Princess, make it comfortable.

It was unbelievable how much he shared with me. He paddled with me on some of my earliest training runs and shared stories about the race while critiquing my form. He told me about getting lost in the lower river and showing up at the Saltwater Barrier at 2 a.m., about eight hours after his team captain expected them. He told me about Owen West, an aging Safari veteran who had competed in all six decades that the race has been held. In 1970, Owen raced tandem with a buddy and they were so frustrated by their leaky canoe that they promptly and ceremoniously burned it upon reaching the finish line in Seadrift. There was only one problem with this dramatic and glorious move; they had borrowed the canoe from a friend.

Above all else, Eric was always positive with me. He kept saying over and over, "You will finish. We are going to make sure you get down that river."

Throughout our year of training, Banning and I marveled at how so many Safari veterans were willing to help. Now, to be clear, not everything in this race is a big lovefest. There are plenty of stories of Safari divorces where teams have gotten crossways and split up, as well as real life divorces, which have also fractured paddling alliances. There have been legendary, longstanding family feuds, as well. But not over moonshine or inbreeding, apparently their fighting started with allegations of cheating and bitter jealousy over winning and losing.

In one notable Safari divorce, a six-man team split up and one faction decided to pull out all the stops to make sure their former partners would never beat them. They went straight to Belize to recruit new teammates since, in these paddling circles, it is well-known that Belizeans are some of the best competitive paddlers in the world. Belizeans are now a fixture in the Safari culture, and it is practically a given that while the bulk of the pack is still hacking away at logjams in the lower Guadalupe, the Belizeans and their Texas teammates will be resting comfortably in Seadrift waiting patiently for the awards banquet to begin.

Watching the hybrid Belizean-Texan team warm up at the start of the race was awe-inspiring, to say the least. They looked like a giant caterpillar, or some massive multi-legged creature straight out of Jurassic Park. All of the appendages moved in perfect coordination while their boat seemed to fly across the surface.

Needless to say we hadn't seen them since the starting line.

With so many fierce and passionate rivalries within the Safari community, Banning and I were surprised that people were so willing to help out a couple of rookies. We talked about it quite a bit on our training runs, and we both agreed that we should be dutiful and gracious listeners, but to also be aware of anything that might not pass the sniff test.

Honestly, though, most people seemed earnestly vested in our success with this race. I suppose the Texas Water Safari simply couldn't continue without fresh recruits. Not only is it time consuming and grueling, it's a niche tradition and if newcomers don't enter the paddling flock year after year, its culture, legacy and the race itself would likely disappear.

Safari veterans were natural mentors. The outreach came from multiple people at various times. Sometimes it was practical, "Come paddle with us on a training run this weekend." Or, "Come over after work and you can see how we've rigged our lighting system." Other times it was more social, "Come, join us at happy hour and we'll share some old race stories." The tone of this recurring descant began to strike a familiar chord. To me, it echoed one of the most classic evangelistic stories of all time, *Come, follow me and I will make you fishers of men.*

But I was starting to hear it as a slightly different refrain. *Come, follow me down this river and I will make you paddlefishers of men.*

Besides Eric, another Team Paddlefish mentor was John Bugge, who was paddling tandem with his girlfriend Meagan. Bugge has competed a staggering 32 times, with 30 finishes, and 27 of those in a row. Not only is Bugge a consistent finisher, he kicks ass. He has won every single category, save Women's Solo, which he is precluded from entering for obvious biological reasons.

Banning and I first met Bugge at his ranch near Luling last

September. Eric and several others recommended that we lease a canoe from Bugge, as he keeps a stockpile of the traditional aluminum models pre-rigged and ready for racing.

Standing in the shadeless dirt next to his barn filled with boats and paddles and gear, Bugge led us in a PhD-level course on the Texas Water Safari. He sized up our boat skills, Banning as an oarsman, and me as a fly fisher with drift boat experience. We discussed reading the water and the mechanics and nuances of proper paddling. He emphasized the importance of maintaining calories, hydration, and keeping the body temperature cool. He stressed the point that if you try to beat the river, you won't finish. You have to work with the river, not against it. He outlined which sections of the river we should conquer first in our training. He spoke of specific obstacles and gave detailed instruction on how to survive them.

I couldn't believe how open he was with so much data and painstaking detail. It was a race, after all, a competitive endeavor. But he was literally giving us the keys to the kingdom.

He then directed the next bit of advice toward me, "Obviously I've never been through child birth, but all the women who race tell me this is harder, longer, and more painful. But similarly it will bring you a lifetime of joy and knowledge. This race is a gift. You will be different after this race."

He turned to Banning, "You both will be different. Just remember, paddle within yourself. Race your own race."

After the verbal briefing, Bugge pointed toward the 17-foot aluminum rental canoe and suggested we give it a whirl. It weighed about eighty pounds, but in one seamless move, he rolled the canoe over with his foot, grabbed it by the gunnels and lifted it upside down over his head without so much as a grunt or a shudder. I was agog. He walked toward his truck, carrying the canoe over his head and loaded it onto the roof rack.

Within a few minutes, Banning and I were paddling down

the San Marcos, euphoric that we were finally making actual progress toward competing in this race.

"Hut!" Phil snapped my mind back to the present.

Mindlessly I switched sides with my paddle. "You know I think Bugge's ranch is somewhere around here. Or no, maybe it's above the Luling takeout?"

"I don't know," Phil shrugged. "When he and Meagan were on that training run last week I didn't see where they got out. We never saw them again after we ran into the logjam."

Phil had been so patient with my crashing us into that tree trunk. Especially since he had to patch the boat at the last minute before the race. I apologized profusely. He just laughed it off and said, "Hey that's just good hard Safari training. It happens. Listen, I'm just impressed that we kept up with Bugge and Meagan as long as we did that day. You know that guy paddles like eighty strokes a minute?"

Even though I kind of missed the aluminum canoe we'd rented from Bugge, I was glad to be in this lighter, faster boat. I can't imagine how heavy the The Beast would have been fully loaded, especially since Banning and I weren't nearly as selective in our gear culling.

"Hut!"

I glanced at my watch at about 6 p.m. hoping for at least a slight drop in temperature. It would be dark in another three hours, but we were making great time. By my calculation, we were within a couple of miles of Zedler Mill, still paddling on fairly easy water, and again my mind began wandering through the past year of training.

The entire ordeal wouldn't have been nearly as much fun if we hadn't befriended the three-woman Hippie Chicks team. Debbie, the unofficial head and heartbeat of the team, already had two Safari finishes. She was an avid outdoor athlete and adventure racer. Janie, Hippie Chick #2, was a Safari novice but she had run marathons and finished at least one Iron Woman competition. The third Hippie

Chick, Ginsie, was a true Safari veteran having raced for years, both solo and with other teams.

In the 2009 Safari, Ginsie went solo and muscled through the low river flows of the Texas drought. She made it all the way into the bay, but was brutally fatigued and disoriented. A Vietnamese fishing boat found her adrift and, instinctively, made its way over to help her. Unfortunately, she was disqualified when they pulled her onto their boat. She had paddled 259 miles and was out of the race within one mile of the finish line.

The Hippie Chicks became dear friends and consistent mentors throughout the spring months. It was nice to have some girls in the mix.

"Hut!"

"I wonder where the fast racers are right now, Bugge, the Hippie Chicks, West and Katie?"

"Gosh, who knows," Phil answered. "Way past Zedler, though. We won't see them until Seadrift. I did hear that the Hippie Chicks weren't planning to sleep until Sunday."

Phil knew all the players in the race scene and had also benefited from a great deal of mentorship. Despite having a Safari patch and finishing in 12th place last year, he always spoke of the veterans with respect. We paddled on toward Zedler chatting lightly about the people in the race as if we were bantering about relatives and whether or not they would be at the family reunion. What time will he arrive? Do you think so-and-so will show? Will there be any food left by the time we get there?

I took another swig of water and shifted in my seat to get centered. If my hips weren't perfectly aligned in this delicate boat, it would throw my whole paddling form off-kilter. When we rounded the next bend the river began to widen and slow, which indicated that the dam at Zedler Mill was close. Thankfully, there was less boat congestion than previous checkpoints as we paddled toward our portage. We had both done this dam several times with other teammates, but we hadn't portaged Zedler together.

The dam stretches across a relatively wide point in the river and has concrete buttresses that angle down to the waterline below. Some racers opted to quickly slide their boats straight down those buttresses, but we chose a more laborious and careful option. At river right, we stopped on a grassy bank and pulled the boat out of the water. It felt odd to stand and use my lower body after six straight miles of sitting and paddling with no portages.

Monica, and our crew met us on a concrete pad to the right of the dam where we exchanged water jugs and ice socks. I waved at Sophie and my mom who stood up on the hill out of the way. As we re-rigged our water tubes and handed off some trash, a race official warned us about the low-water bridge at Palmetto, the next checkpoint.

"Be careful," he cautioned. "There is a sweeper just as you bend river right and the high water is bringing people in really fast as they come up to the checkpoint bridge."

We nodded, appreciative for the information but also focused on getting the boat back down to the water.

Tom and my dad asked about my back. Apparently I had completely freaked them out at Staples when I announced my back was hurt. Truthfully I replied, "Oh yeah, it's fine." They nodded, and I realized I had just learned something that would continue to fascinate me as the race progressed. I learned that the body could actually heal itself in the midst of intense, extended exertion. Miraculously, my back really did feel okay. Of course the lesson I would come to learn later was that the body simply traded the pain from one spot to another.

We surveyed the rocky slope down to the water, trying to pick our best line. We couldn't drag the canoe without damaging the hull, and it was hard to lift it without good footing on the jagged rocks. It was slow going but we eventually crabbed and crawled and inched the boat down the slope. Phil and I communicated well on this portage; we were slowly melding into a common groove.

I waved goodbye to Monica and my family who were standing on the hill, backlit against the evening sun. Their silhouettes waved back, and their cheers were loud. "Go Mommy! Go Phil! Go Team Paddlefish!" We climbed back in the canoe and the other team captains and spectators clapped and cheered as we paddled away toward Palmetto.

## Zedler Mill Checkpoint

| | |
|---|---|
| CUTOFF TIME: | SATURDAY 10:00 P.M. |
| OUR TIME: | SATURDAY 6:35 P.M. |
| PLACE: | 54TH |
| TIME ELAPSED: | 9 HOURS AND 35 MINUTES |
| MILES PADDLED: | 46 |
| MILES TO GO: | 214 |

# CHAPTER 14

# ZEDLER MILL TO PALMETTO

*"Whether you believe you can do a thing or not, you're right."*
–HENRY FORD

Dusk was a good thing. I was thrilled to have the beating sun off my skin, and my headache lessened as the glare off the water subsided. It was still plenty hot but it felt as though the vise grip had loosened slightly. There were fewer boats in view, and it was nice to be able to paddle along without fear of a collision with another team.

Phil called a "hut" and I thought about the next section of the race. We would paddle past the spot where Plum Creek flows into the San Marcos along the border between Caldwell and Gonzales counties. It was on the banks of that tributary that the Texans avenged the Comanche Great Raid with their victory in the 1840 Battle of Plum Creek. They were the most mobile and feared of the raiding Indian tribes, and even though they lived in the plains and canyons of West Texas, the Comanches apparently thought nothing of a 1,000 mile plunder into the heart of the established settlements to their southeast. Ironically, the Texans would have never caught up with the Comanches at Plum Creek had the Indians not been so loaded down with captives, clothing, whiskey, and loot that they had stolen along the way.

I thought about the process of selecting items for our canoe and Eric's sage advice, "Everything weighs something."

*That's right Comanches, ounces turn into pounds.*

As we continued paddling the 14 miles to Palmetto I started browsing my mental file on the obstacles we were about to encounter. First up was a small dam near Ottine. "So, Phil, the next thing we have is Son of Ottine Dam, or Little Ottine. What do you call it?"

"Son of Ottine, I think. Not sure."

"Did y'all run it or portage it in training?"

"I think we ran it. What about you and Banning?"

"Well, the first few times we portaged on the right. But then in higher water we were able to run it straight down the middle. One time the water was so high we didn't even realize we'd paddled over it."

"What do you think we should do?"

"I don't know. It kind of reminds me of Tekins Rapids. I think Banning and I did okay in the aluminum but we might tump in this boat?"

"We'll see when we get closer."

The sun was dropping below the tree line and I began trying to calculate how many hours of night paddling we'd have before we reached Palmetto.

"After Son of Ottine, we have big Ottine Dam, and then the checkpoint at Palmetto."

"Ottine is a pain in the butt portage," Phil said. "They always have a race official there for safety."

"Because of the guy that drowned there?"

"Yeah, that. Plus, there are usually fights that break out there when teams stack up and have to wait on others to portage."

"Wonderful."

The small town of Ottine was named for its founder, Adolf Otto, and his wife Christine. They blended their two names to get Ottine. I, of course, felt an instant attraction to this stretch of the race when I learned I shared the same given name as Christine Otto. The Ottos had naming rights for the town since Adolf built the local gin in 1879 as well as the dam we would portage later that evening.

Near the town is a crescent-shaped oxbow lake adjacent to the main river. Sulfur springs within this swamp helped to create a fertile oasis of vegetation and wildlife. These very springs powered the dam that Adolf Otto built. The Ottine Swamp is the heartbeat of what is now called Palmetto State Park, a 270 acre preservation area. Palmetto State Park is a unique ecosystem, vastly different than the Blackland Prairie and Post Oak Savannah that surround the park area. It is a heavily-wooded swampland with abundant wetland vegetation. Named for the dwarf palmetto plant that grows readily in the park, Palmetto boasts hundreds of other plant species, and over 240 types of birds have been identified there.

This exotic botanical jewel of Central Texas is also home to the legendary Ottine Swamp Monster, referred to locally as "The Thing." Grown men have claimed that they have seen something running through the brush, but whatever it was seemed to be invisible. Campers and hunters claimed The Thing would shake their cars. Ed Sayers in *Ghost Stories of Texas* wrote about Berthold Jackson, an Ottine local who was parked on Lookout Hill with his fiancée when something started pushing their car over the edge. Said Jackson in that memoir:

> *I spent fifty-four months in World War II—Saipan to Okinawa—and the only time in my life that my hair has stood straight on end is when I've looked right at it and couldn't see a thing.*

"Hut!" Phil got my mind off the swamp monster. I wondered

how many times he had said "hut" already. I wondered how many paddle strokes we'd done. By Phil's account, our average stroke rate was probably 50-60 per minute. Since 9 a.m. this morning, that means we had already dipped our paddles at least 30,000 times. That seemed like a lot until I realized that we'd have to stroke at least 200,000 times to reach Seadrift.

Tallying the paddle strokes reminded me that I probably needed some calories. I pulled out a vacuum-packed packet of Pringles and cut into them with my little pair of scissors. I poured the crushed, salty chips in my mouth and chewed slowly while I continued paddling and counting my strokes.

After taking a long swig from my drinking tube, I realized that I could no longer stand the Cytomax electrolyte powder that we were adding to the water jugs. "I am getting sick of this stuff," I told Phil. "I really just want some clean plain water."

"When we get new water jugs at Palmetto, don't add the Cytomax. You'll probably be fine without the electrolytes at night without the sun."

The light was fading fast when we reached Son of Ottine. Compared to what we'd already portaged it was nothing. Actually it was just the remnants of a rocky mill dam, more accurately described as a "weir." As we approached it we couldn't decide whether to run it down the tongue, the seam of water in the middle, or portage on the right.

Phil asked, "Tell me again, how did you and Banning do this?"

"We hugged the right bank and just walked it down the rocky slope in the slower current. I think it's probably our best option."

Phil took my suggestion and steered us toward river right. As we reached the remnants of the old dam, we jumped out of the boat into waist deep water into faster current than I had anticipated. Struggling to control the boat, we eased down through a tangle of rocks and tree roots, but the bow got stuck in the snags. As we

"They offered for me to go ahead since they were taking a while. I didn't care, I was glad for the break. I'm really tired."

"I think we saw you leaving Zedler. You were just a few minutes ahead of us."

The other team was up and gone creating an opening for someone else to portage. Nick was next, then us. Unfortunately we wouldn't see Nick again after Ottine. He apparently stepped out of the race at the Palmetto Checkpoint.

When it was our turn to go, we hustled the boat into position and somehow levered it up the hill and past the Marine boat. Once we crested the plateau, we heard the Marines rustle into place and resume their portage up behind us.

Above the bank there is a long field adjacent to the river. When Banning and I were here a few months before, we had to hack and heave our way through head-high weeds that reminded me of Vietnam War movies.

This time the field wasn't nearly as bad as the thoughtful and Safari-friendly landowner had mowed a path through the jungle for the racers to follow around the dam. When we arrived at the designated spot to portage back down to the river, we found another mob of paddlers waiting in line.

*Good heavens...no wonder fights break out here...*

But everyone was patient and cheering each other softly; the mood was quiet and supportive.

But then the SEMPER FI boat arrived.

With an amped up energy they pushed past us to check out the portage. They were talking loudly about how they were going to get down and who would do what to make it happen.

Phil walked past me and spoke to them politely but firmly, "Listen, when we start heading down this chute, don't start down with your boat until we are out of the way."

They ignored him.

A few seconds later, a younger member of their team came up near us and was looking over the edge. Again Phil said, "Listen you need to tell your team not to start down this thing until we are cleared out of the way. If you drop that boat it'll take us out."

The guy was very nice but replied, "I'll do my best but these guys are pretty fired up. I doubt they're going to want to wait."

At that point I couldn't contain myself, "Listen man, that's no good. Everyone here is waiting for everyone else to finish the portage. How about a little sportsmanship here?"

Phil bristled up and postured toward them and said, "We are about to go. Just wait until we are out of the way before you start."

As the team in front of us cleared down below, we pushed our boat over the ledge and down the chute. Phil started down first, on the left side of the boat. There was an on old rope attached to some trees on the right, presumably placed there ages ago by earlier Safari racers. It was muddy and weathered but I gladly grabbed onto it and dangled along the right side, easing the stern of the canoe down.

Predictably, the Marines started nosing their monster rig over the dirt ledge, looming on top of us. I thought Phil was going to blow a gasket. We perched the boat on some tree roots, each of us making a silent deal with gravity. I remained alone to hold the boat and myself in place on the face of this awkward dirt slide while Phil scrambled back up and told the guy he would kick his ass if he saw that boat move again.

*Whoa, now!*

My partner was taking on six Marines while I was dangling on the side of an eroded piece of earth trying to keep our vertical boat from crashing to the ground. Where the hell was the much-ballyhooed race official who was supposed to be refereeing this debacle?

Thankfully, we portaged the backside of Ottine efficiently and quickly, thus averting a full-on brawl. Until this point, I had actually respected the style and bravado of the Marine team, and their massive homemade boat, which was a bold move, to be sure. They were also racing for charity, which I admired. I would later come to learn that my dad and Tom had befriended their chase team and were eagerly cheering for the Marine boat. Right now, though, they were seriously irritating Phil, and I felt a surge of loyalty toward my partner.

Once we reached the gravel bar at the bottom, it was officially nighttime. We attached the bow light and connected the wires to the battery. We fished out our headlamps from the mesh gear pouch and put them on.

Banning and I never had the chance to do a night run on the San Marcos during our training. We had scheduled one, but unfortunately that's when I came down with bronchitis and we agreed it was risky to lose an entire night's sleep while I was trying to get well. Instead we did a two-hour paddle on the familiar and calm Lady Bird Lake in downtown Austin. It was helpful in that I learned the abilities and limitations of the bow light and my headlamp, but it was meager preparation for night paddling on the San Marcos with all its obstacles.

Much to my surprise, I found that I liked night paddling. Obviously the lack of sun was a gift. It was still sticky and hot at night, but it was really nice to have a break from the blazing heat. Plus being in the bow, I now had a defined role that kept my mind occupied. Like that lonely young fellow long ago that didn't see a giant iceberg until it was too late, my job in the crow's nest was to look for—and point out—oncoming rocks, stumps, and branches.

*I hope we fare better than the Titanic.*

Once we switched on the lights, it didn't take all that long for my eyes to adjust. The headlamps marginalized the effectiveness of the bow lamp, so we only turned them on when we needed to look at something off to the right or left. Obviously the mounted bow light only illuminated what lay dead ahead.

With diminished visibility, it was also crucial to rely more on our ears. Light *swishing* sounds, might indicate a branch hanging in the water, or maybe a stump to avoid. Louder *swooshing* sounds could be small sets of rapids. We could hear turtles bailing off logs with a distinctive *blurp*, and birds cheeping and cawing from their nighttime roosts. The scratching and rustling noises in the surrounding foliage weren't particularly helpful, but they added to the aura of night paddling.

A couple of miles before the Palmetto Checkpoint we were stroking along in eerie black silence when a loud THUD sounded from our portside bow. On the edge of our light beam I caught the flash and roll of the massive gar that whacked our bow before it slipped beneath the surface. The impact rocked our delicate alignment and it took a bit of shifting and trimming to get our hips back on center.

Remembering the warning we'd received from race officials, Phil took the lead in discussing our strategy for Palmetto.

"When we come up to the checkpoint, I want you to jump out of the boat on the right side where the current is slower. Get to the bank quickly so you can run up on the low water bridge. I will steer the boat to the bridge and you can be there to catch me. Then I'll jump up and we'll pull it over the bridge together."

"Cool. So when we come around that big bend curving to the left the checkpoint pops up really quickly. Are you concerned about the water moving too fast?"

"We should be fine."

We did come around the bend with some speed, but we were ready. It was wild to see the scene on the low water bridge at night. The bridge was lined with dark silhouettes of bodies, flashing safety lights, race officials, and team captains with headlamps. There were boats lined up and racers clamoring to get their canoes out of the water as quickly as possible. Once again I wondered how Monica and our crew would find us, but once again they were right where we needed them to be.

We slowed down and angled toward river right. When we reached the bank I secured my paddle so it wouldn't get lost in the shuffle. When Phil shouted for me to get out I did my best to follow his instructions from training: up and over the edge without leaning on the side, and let go of the bow quickly to keep the stern from spinning around. I waded over to the bank and jogged along the muddy edge toward the bridge. Monica, Tom and my dad were waiting there in the exact place where we planned to pull out the boat.

After the race my dad and Tom would both talk about how remarkable the Palmetto Checkpoint experience was. Nightfall had created a dramatic overlay for the chase team just as it had for us. They had been out there with their headlamps, looking upriver for us while we'd been looking downriver for obstacles. All they could see were the pinpricks of light coming toward the bridge, only recognizing faces in the boat at the final moment. Apparently many boats struggled to get over the bridge efficiently and the race officials, particularly worried about the safety at this checkpoint, had established a poignant sense of gravitas. Water lapped over the bridge at times. There was chaos with very little room to operate, but our crew had staked out a good spot to ensure we would have room on the bridge once we arrived.

Palmetto went well for Team Paddlefish. I was up on the bridge, as planned, when Phil guided the bow right to me. I cushioned it from driving into the concrete ledge while he jumped out and climbed up next to me. In a well-choreographed move we lifted the boat out of the water, avoided losing it under the bridge, and collected our new water jugs from Monica. We didn't need ice socks this time of night, so we just handed our trash off in a hurry. As quickly as possible we lifted our boat off the back side of the bridge and paddled away from the mayhem. I could hear Tom cheering behind us as we took off.

We left the Palmetto Checkpoint just two minutes after the Marine boat. While we would continue to leapfrog with them a little while longer, in the next section of the river they would ignite their afterburners and peel away from us for good. I knew it was stressful for Phil to navigate and steer around them, especially in the narrow stretches, but I actually missed the Marines. They were good competition, comparable rivals. That is, until they picked up their pace and ditched us.

## Palmetto Checkpoint

| | |
|---|---|
| CUTOFF TIME: | SUNDAY 10:00 A.M. |
| OUR TIME: | SATURDAY 10:02 P.M. |
| PLACE: | 54TH |
| TIME ELAPSED: | 13 HOURS AND 2 MINUTES |
| MILES PADDLED: | 60 |
| MILES TO GO: | 200 |

# CHAPTER 15

# PALMETTO TO SLAYDEN

*"Now I see the secret of making the best persons, it is to grow in the open air and to eat and sleep with the earth."*
−WALT WHITMAN

My first night of paddling the Water Safari was long and surreal. We pulled away from Palmetto just after 10 p.m., hoping to get somewhere near Gonzales before stopping to rest.

Phil shared his thoughts, "I'd rather not sleep at the Gonzales Checkpoint. It's just so noisy there. Plus, that's where all the homeschoolers have their all-night prayer groups, it can get kinda loud."

"Prayer groups?"

"Yeah there's a big network of Christian families—homeschoolers—that race in the Safari. The race has been passed down through their families for generations. They are very religious and incredible racers. They train hard and are really disciplined. It's like religion and the Safari are everything to these families."

"What about the prayer groups?"

"Oh yeah, well, when the racers from these families reach Gonzales in the middle of the first night, they go up the hill with their team captains and sing songs and have prayer meetings."

"Well if it's too noisy when we arrive, then let's definitely find a better spot."

"Hut!"

I listened while I paddled and kept my focus straight ahead. I was searching for tree stumps. We were only one night away from the new moon, which meant we had zero ambient light. It was dark. Humid and dark. And stumps were much harder to see than icebergs. No matter how hard I scanned the waterline in front of us, they would still often materialize too suddenly to react. We brushed against a lot of them, and hit a couple head on, but none of those collisions damaged the boat. Luckily my draw stroke seemed to be improving, and I exercised them on my own initiative multiple times to avoid a stump or branch in the water. More moral victories.

There seemed to be a collective sigh among other teams on the river as we all paddled south from Palmetto. If not a sigh of relief, perhaps just resignation that we were all settling into the long night ahead. Boats were spreading out and there were no longer throngs of spectators crowding the bridges and dangling from trees.

By our estimation, Team Paddlefish was traveling in the middle of the race pack at this point. The real contenders were pushing ahead at lightning speed. Those that were struggling to make the checkpoint cutoff times were behind us. But we were starting to establish ourselves among a pack.

We paddled for a while with a father and son team, Jamie and Brian.

"I like your boat," Phil remarked to them.

"Yeah, it's a good one," Jamie, the father, answered. "This is Brian's first Safari and the boat's working out well for us."

"This is Christine's first Safari, too. This one's fairly stable, but we have a low freeboard, should be interesting in the bay. We might take on too much water."

I chimed in and asked Brian what he thought about the race, so far.

He sort of nodded and shrugged his shoulders at the same time, "Pretty wild."

Jamie continued, "I've done the Safari several times, I just love it. I think it's the coolest thing. I've been trying to get Brian to do it with me for awhile."

While Jamie and Phil continued to talk about boats and paddles and rudders (we had a rudder, they didn't) I thought about how great it was that a father and son were sharing such a monumental undertaking.

I can't remember who pulled away from whom, at that point, but we leapfrogged with Jamie and Brian a number of times. It was always a treat to see them on the race course. They were strong paddlers, mellow guys, and pleasant conversation.

At around 10:30 p.m. we ran into a solo paddler that Phil knew.

His name was Charlie and when Phil called out to him in the dark, he seemed confused as to who we were.

"It's Phil, and this is Christine."

"Oh, hey. Phil, I thought you were going solo?"

"Christine lost her partner with the delay. So I decided to race with her. How's it going?"

"Well, it'd be better if my rudder wasn't broken."

"Yikes, that's no good."

In a glorious Safari moment that rivaled something Mac-Gyver would have pulled off, Charlie Stewart would later scavenge the metal door off a discarded animal trap that he found near the river. With whatever minimal toolkit he had onboard, he fashioned a replacement rudder blade from the old trap door and affixed it to the bracket on his stern. One man's trash is a Safari paddler's salvation.

Eric Wilder had told me early on that you have to take everything you need for the race, but you can use any trash or anything you find in the river if you need it. I chewed on that for a while as we paddled on in silence and thought about what debris I might find that would be useful. The Dairy Queen cups, dirty diapers, and livestock carcasses that we often saw littering the riverbanks seemed of little practical use.

*A paddle maybe? If I lost a paddle and then found one floating down the river, that would be useful. Or a pillow. A nice dry fluffy pillow would be great right now...*

We pushed on through the eerie blackness with turtles diving from logs and gar continually lashing at our bow light. The tree frog chorus was loud and the absence of a moon allowed the stars to burn extra bright.

Around 11 p.m., our conversation turned to wildlife, and I told Phil about my favorites of all of the animals Banning and I had seen on our training runs: the bobcat speeding along the bank below San Marcos in broad daylight, and the gang of feral hogs swimming across the river near Zedler. These weren't little pink farm pigs. They were massive black and brown feral swine with thick wiry hair and huge barrel bodies with teeny little legs. We paddled into a herd of about thirty of them crossing the river. I was amazed they could even stay afloat, but they glided through the water with ease, poking their iconic pig noses just above the surface. We assumed they'd have trouble when they reached the near vertical bank, but they clambered up the muddy slope like bighorn sheep on a craggy rock face.

"I haven't seen an alligator yet while training, have you?"

"We will," Phil responded. "Especially below Victoria."

"That's what everyone tells me."

"Hut."

As the night wore on, we noticed other teams starting to bed down here and there along the banks. Sometimes we'd hear, "Looking good Paddlefish." Or, "Hey Team Paddlefish! See you in Seadrift!" Or, a friend of Phil's would call out, "Good job Phil."

Around 11:30 p.m. I popped another chocolate electrolyte goo packet from my collection that was zip-tied under the bow. I washed it down with a long sip of clean water from my drinking tube. It tasted so good to be free of the Cytomax, I drank more. And more still.

After another stretch of silent paddling, I began to mull over one of my remaining unresolved apprehensions about this race. My number one concern was where to go number two. Could I skip that program for three or four days? That didn't sound very healthy, or comfortable. Despite many people proclaiming it "the Safari way," there was absolutely no scenario on this planet, in this lifetime, or in hell where this Honeybear would go in the river, *or* the woods.

While I may not be as, shall we say, *bold* as some of the female Safari veterans, I've done some time in the outdoors, and the grungy river life doesn't freak me out one bit, but my past outdoor latrine experiences have involved…well…actual latrines.

The first time I floated Montana's Smith River with my parents, I was nervous about the bathroom facilities on a five-day float trip, not to mention the logistics of shaving my legs on that showerless journey.

We were booked with one of the best outfitters in Montana, and they had a tight program. Each day while we fished, the tents were set up with cots and sleeping bags, delicious meals were prepared, and the boats and the gear were handled at every turn. Luxurious by many standards to be sure, but all outdoor adventures exist on a continuum of challenge depending on the individual involved, and I was still curious about those potties.

A latrine on the Smith is not a traditional campsite outhouse, mind you. The state has built alfresco commodes at each campsite in the canyon. Sometimes they're close to the river, sometimes up a hill, and occasionally you'll find the throne in a wide-open field. It's literally a toilet seat perched atop a wooden box that covers a hole in the ground where deposits are made. No walls for privacy or protection from the elements.

During our trip orientation, one of the veteran guides launched into his standard spiel about the campsite bathroom system. Waving a roll of toilet paper encased in a Ziploc bag he pointed into the woods and simply said, "When it comes to the latrines there are two rules. One: don't look down, and two: enjoy the view."

Let's just say I broke the first rule right out of the gate and put my gag reflexes to the ultimate test. I marched up to the latrine and looked straight down.

*Oh my God, what have these people been eating? Who is responsible for that and are they on my trip? Did I eat that too?*

Thankfully, the fishing took center stage and I soon forgot about the latrines. I didn't exactly relish the experience of going to the toilet box, but I was less disturbed with each visit. I hadn't looked into the hole since the first day, but it wasn't until the last night of the trip that I fully understood Rule #2. I was perched atop the latrine on the banks of the Smith River, the sun was setting and I could hear the laughter of my friends and family in camp. Out of nowhere this beautiful eagle soared right over my head leaving me breathless and totally in awe.

Okay so I'm not entirely sure it was an eagle; it could have been a buzzard. But it was large and majestic and it created one of those transcendental moments in nature when you feel an overwhelming sense of gratitude, and a wave of calm that can only be replicated in daily life with prescription medication.

Looking back, the lessons that I learned on that trip basically mirrored our guide's initial instructions: life's blessings often come in the most unexpected places, and you should never ever involve yourself in other people's shit.

Oh by the way, I also learned that if you take a battery-operated razor on a group camping trip, you should use it out in the open for all to see because if someone walks by your tent while you're inside shaving your legs, it *does not* sound like a razor. Being the only one at the end of the trip with silky smooth legs was apparently not enough evidence to spare me from unmitigated mockery.

"Hut."

About eight miles below the Palmetto Checkpoint we came upon the Slayden Cemetery Bridge. It was a high narrow bridge, and there were silhouettes of the faithful, team captains and essential support crew, outlined against the night sky. I knew I wouldn't see Sophie and my mom again until morning. They were probably sound asleep in air-conditioned motel comfort, while Tom and my dad kept up their river vigil with Monica.

As we paddled a line that would take us directly under the center of the bridge, I noticed something large and white dangling at eye level.

"Phil...do you see—?"

"I do...what the *hell* is that?"

A woman on the bridge was dangling a bucket from a rope and yelling down to us, "Can you reach that? Is that a good height? Hey! Hey! Can you reach that?"

We weren't sure if they were trying to give us something and Phil warned, "Don't touch it." He didn't want us to get disqualified over some odd shenanigan.

One of the women yelled in a more demanding tone, "Can you reach that?"

We were just about to paddle under the bridge and the bucket was right in my face. I didn't bother to answer but had to lean left to avoid hitting it.

Phil shouted back up, "Yeah we can reach it. Now MOVE it!"

We paddled a few more feet and I asked, "What was that all about?"

"I guess some team captain was trying to come up with a new way to get water to their racers."

"Seems like they're over-engineering things."

We heard them focus grouping their bucket-on-a-rope program with another unsuspecting team behind us. For some reason it really irritated me. How did they even expect their own team to stop in the center current of the river and stay still under the bridge long enough to take their water in and out of the bucket?

I wondered if there was something besides water in there. Since this race first began, there have been consistent rumors and allegations of cheating, mostly involving team captains handing contraband items to their racers in covert locations between the checkpoints. Certainly they wouldn't be so brazen as to literally wave a double cheeseburger and fries in the faces of other racers?

Would they?

Over the years, those same accusations have resulted in continual tweaking and tightening of the race rules. I suppose it's no different than a fishing tournament where someone gets caught shoving lead weights down the gullets of their catch. Paddling, like fishing, has become competitive, and some will unfortunately resort to cheating when pride and ego are mixed with the possibility of winning a substantial prize.

Or a patch.

# CHAPTER 16

# SLAYDEN TO GONZALES

*"I thought I knew Texas pretty well, but I had no notion of its size until I campaigned it."*
—FORMER TEXAS GOVERNOR ANN RICHARDS

We passed a few boats after Slayden and a few passed us. Mostly, though, we paddled alone in the blackness of the river corridor.

Just before midnight we saw a boat up ahead in the gloom. Without saying it aloud, we both paddled harder to try and gain on them. It was a psychological boost to have a goal. We were making some progress on closing the gap, but then they seemed to vanish along the right side of the river. Like an apparition that wisped away, they were just gone in the dark. As we paddled closer we saw why.

"Whoa, big log jam!" I yelled out to Phil.

"What do you see? Any way through?"

"I'm looking but I can't see any gaps. Those guys must have gone through on the right but I can't see where."

We slowed down our pace so as not to come up on it too fast. Water could be rushing under the trees and logs and we didn't want to get sucked under that mess. The big logjams were incredible, spanning the river from one bank to the other and often reaching twenty feet high.

Phil said, "This is tricky. The banks are so steep here, there's no way to take the boat out and portage around it."

We inched up on the left side and used our headlamps to look into the tangle.

"Phil, I don't see any opening over here."

With our paddles, we traversed toward the right side of the massive pile.

"What do you see in there? What do you think?"

Tentatively, I replied, "I think this is where that other boat went through...this may be our only choice."

Trusting me, Phil gave the signal to paddle hard so we could clear some logs and branches that were at water level. It was wild to go through this quagmire at night, but almost better not to see all the junk that was clinging to branches and collecting in small foaming pools. Since we were still near towns and cities, it was a junkyard of litter—human and animal. Styrofoam cups, thick cobwebs of goo, and the remains of unidentifiable critters that washed in among the tangled mass of trees. I decided to stop paying attention when my headlamp illuminated a nasty latex glove swirling among an eddy of leaves.

We paddled hard over logs in an effort to stay in the boat. As we tunneled through the thicket, I covered my face to protect my eyes from branches and leaves. At one point we had to lie flat on our backs and use our hands to pull ourselves through like kids on monkey bars. If we got stuck on a log, one of us would get out, stand on a lower log below water level, and push us off and forward. Amazingly, in the pitch black we picked our way through the nastiness without any major problems.

"Okay now *that* was gross."

"No kidding," Phil agreed. "That's the kind of logjam where you have to worry about a hypodermic needle or something really creepy."

After clearing that mess, Phil and I discussed the rumored massive logjams in the lower race course. Last year during the drought there was a huge logjam below the Dupont Checkpoint that required a one-mile portage. Lots of paddlers were asking about it this week before our race began, but details and intel were sketchy.

Just after the logjam the urge to pee came upon me suddenly. I had drunk quite a bit of water in the last couple of hours, and there hadn't been any impromptu swims that would offer a pee break.

I paddled on and held my urge, hoping Phil would have to go eventually and would initiate a river dip. But he never did.

After another seemingly very long stretch of paddling, I finally spoke up. "Phil, I'm so sorry but I have to pee."

"Okay. Well, we can't really just stop right here. It's deep and the water is moving pretty fast. Since it's so dark and we can't really see what's beneath the surface you probably should go on land to be safe."

At that point the pressing urge became a full-on crisis. "Phil, I could go in the boat."

"Nope. No peeing in the boat. That's my one rule."

"Can't you just run the bilge pump?"

Amused but unwavering, "No. No peeing in the boat."

We switched on our headlamps and scanned the impenetrable wall of foliage on the high banks. No pee spots. Just little illuminated tiny yellow eyeballs here and there.

*Raccoons? Opossums? Swamp monsters? Who cares, I just need to pee...*

It was starting to hurt really bad. Good heavens, I didn't want to die of a bladder explosion. What would they tell Sophie? I would certainly become an urban legend that's mentioned in every Safari orientation seminar for all eternity.

*In 2010 a woman from Austin died when her bladder...*

I tried to think positive thoughts. But every time Phil called a hut and I had to switch to paddle on the opposite side, it awakened the giant sleeping urine monster in my bladder.

"Phil, this is getting serious!"

He laughed, "I know, but all these banks are too steep."

We had paddled past hundreds of gravel bars in the past 13 hours, and now we couldn't find one.

"Next time you have to go give me more of a heads-up before it's so urgent. It's not always easy to find a good bank when you need it."

"Lessons later, Phil! I can't learn anything new right now! There is a serious real estate issue going on here. My entire body is filled with urine, even my brain."

Phil seemed entertained by my plight and his laughter lightened the overall mood.

After an eternity we finally found a low bank and I literally launched myself from the canoe and into the bushes. I'm not sure I've ever enjoyed a bathroom break that much in my life.

From the river Phil shouted, "That's a good sign. At least you're not dehydrated!"

Midnight came and went, and before we knew it, it was tomorrow. Unceremoniously, we paddled on. It didn't feel like Sunday out there in the pitch black, but it was. It didn't really feel like any day of the week at all.

Getting out of the boat had awakened me a bit. I was able to stretch my legs and get the blood flowing in my lower body. It didn't hurt anymore but I was still nervous about my back.

But the energy boost faded quickly.

*How much further to Gonzales?*

I snacked and I drank, but I was starting to zone out. Conversation slacked off. The trees towered over us from each side of the river. The sliver of sky we could see up above seemed to be getting even blacker. We paddled for another hour in silence.

At about 1 a.m. Phil suggested we pull over for a nap. Again it took at least a half-hour to find a suitable place. Finally we found a nice flat bank at river left.

We lugged the boat completely out of the water so it wouldn't inadvertently travel on to Seadrift without us. I turned off the bow light immediately so as not to attract more insects than necessary. Of course, when we switched on our headlamps, those gnats, moths and mosquitoes that were buzzing around the bow light immediately moved to our faces. I closed my mouth and sealed my lips, not caring that some Safari vets joked about bugs being a good source of protein.

We secured our paddles then grabbed our life vests and Ridgerest pads. We hiked about twenty feet up the bank and found a nice, flat clearing. Perfect! I spread out my sleeping pad and dropped my life vest down as a pillow.

As quickly as I got seated on the ground I clicked off my headlamp to keep the bugs away. I ran my hand over my clothes and picked off burrs and little sticks, annoying souvenirs from the log-jam. I patted my hair and felt all sorts of debris in there as well. I slid my hand over my braid and found it still intact.

Phil was settling on to his foam pad about the same time and called over, "Be sure to take your shoes off. This is the only chance your feet will have to dry out during the whole race."

I took off my shoes and my feet glowed like a white-hot ember in the night. Out of morbid curiosity I had to turn my headlamp back on to look at them. The skin was white, bright white, and it was all crinkled up and gritty looking. My feet were completely unrecognizable as my own.

I placed my shoes and my headlamp to the side and set the alarm on my wristwatch for one hour. It was an out of body experience to lay my hot, weary body down flat. I felt like I was still gently rocking on the water. I was grateful for the Ridgerest pad but it didn't exactly mask the hard lumpy ground beneath me—plus, it was only long enough for my hips and upper body so my legs dangled in the dirt and gravel.

Through the fatigued haze in mind, I stared up at the stars for a bit and then closed my eyes. For a nanosecond I swung back to full alert, panicked that a snake would slither right over my face, but that thought passed quickly and I fell asleep hard.

Unfortunately, my deep restorative slumber only lasted about twenty minutes.

Mosquitoes were buzzing around my face, so I pulled up my Buff to cover my ears, nose and eyes. Strange as it seemed in the heat of July in Texas, I was chilled and shivering. I had been warned that this would happen. When a person expends so much energy, burning lots of calories for hours on end, the body will rapidly begin to dump heat as soon as it becomes still and inactive. My damp muddy clothes didn't help the matter. I curled up in a ball, trying to hold on to any body heat I could generate…

And the noises!

Crunch crunch. Scratch scratch. Crickets chirping, tree frogs croaking. I was beginning to feel the sounds of nature were completely overrated.

I drifted in and out for another fifteen minutes or so. I could hear Phil turning over on his mat, as well, obviously not fully asleep.

"Christine?"

"Yeah?"

"I think we should get going."

We sat up, still groggy, and gathered up our gear.

On the one hand, I was bummed. This nap wasn't nearly long enough. On the other hand, it wasn't exactly working out and I wanted to cover some river miles. If we couldn't sleep, then maybe we could kill some tree frogs along the way for sport.

At around 3:30 a.m., we reached the northern outskirts of Gonzales and the spot where the San Marcos reaches the end of its 81-mile run.

"Wow, we have just paddled the full length of the San Marcos," I shared softly.

"Yeah, we're on the Guadalupe."

"And we made it in one piece."

"Yep."

It was an achievement we were too tired to celebrate properly. We paddled on and I started to enjoy the magnitude of our new course. The Guadalupe is a bigger river with a commanding presence. It was wide and slow, but at least we didn't have tree stumps coming at us from every angle. I relaxed in my half-awake existence and took it all in. Everything seemed even bigger in the middle of the night. Or maybe I just felt smaller. The pecan trees were massive and abundant along the banks. The stars seemed bigger. Everything towered over me, especially the task at hand.

After another long stretch of silent paddling, Phil piped in from the stern, "Tell me a story."

I didn't have the energy to respond.

Then he said it again, "Tell me a story."

I racked my brain but couldn't think of anything. I was an English major and studied creative writing. I love telling stories and I'm rarely at a loss for words, but at that point my mind was a blank slate.

"Tell me a story."

"Oh my gosh, Phil, I can't think of one. How about we sing instead?"

"Singing is good."

It was obvious that Phil and I had never spent any time at the same beer joints listening to the same jukeboxes because we didn't know one lick of each other's music. He would sing a few lines of something, and I would have to fess up, "I have no idea, I've never heard that song."

I sang a few Willie Nelson tunes, Janis Joplin. No go.

For some reason I started singing, "You are the woman that I've always dreamed of..."

Phil joined in with, "I knew it from the start..."

In chorus, "I saw your face and that's the last I've seen of my heart!"

Who would have guessed that soft rock of the 70s would be the genre that would get us downriver? After we beat Firefall into the ground we moved on. Team Paddlefish was firing on all jukebox cylinders. From there we belted through every verse (we could remember) from Don McLean's *American Pie*, *Take it Easy* by the Eagles, *Life's Been Good* by Joe Walsh, and everyone's favorite, *Country Roads* by John Denver.

We sang for about three miles until the river widened and slowed and we knew it was time to keep an eye out for the Gonzales Dam. At 4:30 a.m. we paddled beneath the cable hanging across the river that holds a sign warning not to pass that point. We proceeded well past that point and angled right, looking for our portage spot.

Built in the early 1900s, the Gonzales Dam is essential for flood control and also provides hydroelectric power to the city.

As portages go, it's a bitch.

Standing about 15 feet high there is usually a rushing torrent of water coming over its top, even during normal flows. A few months back, on a scouting run, Banning and Tosh and I were standing next to the dam when a bloated and very dead cow came cascading over the top. At that point we still weren't sure how to portage it, but we knew that the Holstein Line wasn't the best option.

Nervous about getting too close to the dam, Phil and I began scanning the right bank for the blinking yellow light that the race officials usually install to mark the portage spot.

"Phil, why don't we just get out here? I think Banning and I pulled the boat out in that opening, I remember that weird sideways tree root."

"Let's just see..."

We paddled in slow motion, scanning the bank. Perhaps it

was my perspective in the front of the boat, but it seemed we were getting awfully close to the edge of the dam. I abandoned the search for the safety light on the right bank and locked my gaze straight ahead on the lip of water crashing over the dam. I took a deep breath, and committed to trusting Phil. Trust Phil. Trust my partner.

*Screw Phil. I have to trust my instincts! He's tired. He could make a mistake! I'm a mother, I cannot die going over the Gonzales dam.*

I picked a spot on the water and decided if we reached it, I would jump out of the boat. I watched intently as the bow of the boat inched closer.

"Here it is!"

*Oh thank heavens.*

The blinking yellow safety light would have been easier to see had it not been wedged between two tree trunks. It was a meager safety measure for such a major threat.

As we pulled over to the right, anxious to get the boat out of the water, there was a racer already trying to make the ascent up the steep bank. Phil and I were both surprised that we hadn't seen him. We scooted in tight to the bank, said "hey" to him quietly, and grabbed onto some tree roots to hold ourselves in place.

We waited while he finished his portage. It was clear he'd already been at it awhile. He was a solo racer, and somehow had already managed to position his boat vertically against the steep bank. As we watched in silence, he stood thigh-deep in the water and tried to climb up the muddy bank so he could pull his boat out. He was obviously worn out and having trouble finding natural leverage points to help him climb the bank. He tried several times, but he kept sliding back down with his face and torso against the dirt wall. It was demoralizing to watch a grown man struggle like this, moaning into the night. His groans sounded desperate, not grunts of progress and output.

After another agonizing effort he finally made it up to a ledge where he could stand upright. After catching his breath, he pulled his boat up and out of the way. We prepared for our turn.

We got out of the boat in hip-deep water and worked it into vertical position. Phil climbed up first and made certain it was lodged against a tree for support.

"Can you get up okay? Do you need a hand?"

"I think I can do it. Let me see."

I found a place to put my foot on a tree root, then found another root up above that I could reach well enough to get some leverage. Pushing hard with my legs I hoisted myself up and flopped over the edge of the high bank. It was something of a beached whale maneuver but at least I made it up the first time.

After dragging the boat the rest of the way up, Phil suggested we take a few minutes to look around and scout the best way to portage down. We walked through a dark, heavily wooded area and came out near the rocky slope that angled down from the top of the dam to the river, below.

"That looks tough," Phil said.

"Banning and I got the aluminum canoe down those boulders, but our boat might be too delicate."

Phil pointed at the muddy ground, "These are canoe tracks. From people dragging their boats. Maybe there's a better place to get back down to the river if we follow these."

We walked along the high bank, following some distinct canoe tracks, but couldn't find a place where previous racers would have dropped back in."

"Where's that solo guy?" Phil asked.

"No clue."

"You'd think we would have seen him again."

Preferring not to carry the boat too far without a solid plan, we decided to backtrack and take the boulder route. As seamlessly as we powered the boat up and out of the water, we battled desperately to get it back down to the river. We had to inch it along carefully down the slope of jagged rocks, and all the while worry about breaking the canoe, an ankle, or a shinbone. It took considerably longer than we had expected, and we were completely beat down when we finally reached the bank below the dam. Phil would later say his morale was at its lowest at this point.

When we finally got down to the soft back-eddy below, we again looked around for the solo guy, but it was like he had vaporized. We never saw him again. Looking back, it was strange that he had so much trouble going up the bank, while we had foundered badly going down. That was the essence of the Texas Water Safari. One minute you're depleted, the next you're a Herculean hero. You can go over from frontrunner to DNF in the blink of an eye. I suppose with this race, as with life, everyone struggles at different points.

Physically and mentally drained, we limped along for another half-mile, past the golf course and Independence Park where a sign proclaims "Welcome to Gonzales, The Birthplace of Texas."

Just before we reached the Gonzales Checkpoint, Phil remarked, "I am so glad I didn't do this race solo. Watching that guy do that portage just made it so clear to me. Going solo would be so boring, for one thing. But watching that guy try to get that boat up? I don't know how I would have done that portage by myself."

A sense of validation swelled inside of me. While Phil was clearly physically stronger than I was, he genuinely felt I had contributed in that grueling portage. Of course, I missed Banning. I wasn't sure I would ever understand why I wasn't meant to do this race with him after all we'd been through to prepare. But Phil and I were finally starting to gel as teammates, away from the shadow of my former partnership with Banning, and away from the negative taste Phil still had for his former team and their falling out.

Maybe Phil needed me to race with him just as much as I needed him to race with me. Who knows the reasons why we pass in and out of someone's life at a certain time? But I believe that there is a reason. And it's part of a plan that's bigger than this race. Bigger, even, than Texas.

Just up the hill from the gravel bar at the Gonzales Checkpoint there is a Historical Marker that reads:

*On this site, September 29 1835, began the strategy of the 18 Texians who by advising with Alcade Andrew Ponton, held for two days 150 Mexican Dragoons sent to demand the Gonzales cannon, allowing colonists time to mass recruits for the Battle of Gonzales.*

After two days, as the Texans stalled, made excuses, and built up their fighting force, the Mexicans again demanded the return of their cannon, to which the Texans replied, "Come and take it!" The ensuing battle ended when the Texans aimed that same cannon at the advancing forces and touched off a booming blast of scrap metal. The Mexicans retreated to San Antonio, and the Texans got to keep the cannon, and their pride.

As far as military battles go, the Battle of Gonzales was not much more than a skirmish. But its political significance was poignant as it galvanized the Texans' opposition to Santa Anna. Six months later, in March of 1836, tempers flared again when Santa Anna found 187 Texans defiantly holding their ground in a little stone mission in San Antonio called The Alamo.

We arrived at the Gonzales Checkpoint at about 5:40 a.m. Sunrise was just over an hour away and the sky was beginning to lighten. We paddled silently up to the gravel bar right where Monica and my dad were sitting in two folding chairs. It was a quiet and subdued scene. There were a number boats on the gravel bar and racers napping on their sleeping pads up on the hill. Monica sprang into action when she saw us and turned to wake up my dad.

"No," I whispered. "Not necessary."

"He would not want to miss you." She was always so upbeat,

"How are y'all doing? How was your night on the river?"

Phil answered softly, "Fine. No need to rush with the water jugs or anything. We're gonna lay down for a bit."

"Where's Tom?" I asked Monica.

"Getting some rest at the motel. He and your dad decided to trade off in shifts."

At that point my dad awoke and jumped from his chair.

"Hey! Y'all doing okay?"

"Yeah fine, Daddy, we're gonna rest."

As we handed over some trash to Monica, one of the Water Safari officials came over and logged in our official time. Affably, he then pointed at me and said, "What's with you? You're like the dirtiest person I've seen in this whole race. Is Phil making you do all the work?"

I looked down and laughed. My formerly white shirt and tights were a dingy gray and marked with brown streaks. Most of it was mud from my graceful bank-climbing escapades, but some of it was melted chocolate from my Clif bars.

We grabbed our Ridgerest pads and life vests and asked Monica to wake us if we were still asleep in an hour. We walked about thirty feet up to a grassy slope, and laid down to rest. Once again I fell asleep fast. Once again, I didn't stay asleep long. I could hear Phil tossing and turning not far from me. I didn't dare let him see I was awake for fear we'd have to leave right away. So I rolled over to face the other way. Thankfully there were no frogs at this spot, but there were plenty of croaking humans. I nodded off again but woke when another team arrived and bedded down in the grass to the right of us. They made considerable noise opening their space blankets which crinkled like a bag of Doritos.

After another half hour or so of fitful sleep, Phil and I roused to face the day. He announced he was heading over to the port-a-potty.

"Are we allowed to use those?" I asked.

"Oh yeah. They're for all the racers and Safari people."

I couldn't believe it. How was I just now hearing about this? After all the research and interviews and advice I'd gathered to prepare for this race, no one ever told me there were port-a-potties at the checkpoints that we could use. Knowing that Phil didn't like to hang around the checkpoints, I took advantage of what might be my last chance to use a bathroom with four walls.

The port-a-potty wasn't all that disgusting. Not nearly as crude and odiferous as the ones on the Smith River. But nature wasn't working with me the way I needed it too. I really didn't want to have to go big later in the day without a port-a-potty, so I did some divine bargaining, asking God and the homeschoolers to please help me get things moving.

Thankfully my prayers were finally answered, but I knew Phil would be tapping his toe, so I hustled out of there as quickly as possible. The sun was up and sure enough Phil was standing in the water by our boat, thoroughly frustrated. "What's going on? We have to get out of here."

"I know. I'm here."

"I mean we have to get moving, I was just talking to my friend who is one of the officials and he says we need to get moving because the water level is dropping."

I got out my paddle and started putting on my hat and sunglasses. "Okay, I'm here, let's go."

"What were you doing? I mean when this water drops, we lose our ride to Seadrift. We need to ride the current down there, it makes a huge difference."

"Oh my gosh, what is wrong with you? I'm right here. Let's go!"

"I was just—"

"Listen Phil. I was in the port-a-potty. Do you think I enjoy hanging out in plastic outhouses that have been fermenting in the

Texas heat? Do you? Do you actually think I wanted to be in there? So logically, if I am in a port-a-potty, you can rest assured there is a reason."

"All I'm saying is we need to go."

"Oh my gosh, already. So let's go!"

And thus began Team Paddlefish's second day in the Texas Water Safari.

## Gonzales Checkpoint

| | |
|---|---|
| CUTOFF TIME: | SUNDAY 5:00 P.M. |
| OUR TIME: | SUNDAY 6:40 A.M. |
| PLACE: | 52ND |
| TIME ELAPSED: | 21 HOURS AND 40 MINUTES |
| MILES PADDLED: | 85 |
| MILES TO GO: | 175 |

# CHAPTER 17

# GONZALES TO HOCHHEIM

*"Every morning in Africa, a gazelle wakes up.*
*It knows it must outrun the fastest lion or it will be killed.*
*Every morning in Africa, a lion wakes up. It knows it must run*
*faster than the slowest gazelle, or it will starve. It doesn't matter*
*whether you're a lion or a gazelle–when the sun comes up,*
*you'd better be running."*

–SIR ROGER BANNISTER

When we pulled away from the Gonzales Checkpoint, the sun was already bright in the sky. My body felt okay but my eyes struggled to adjust to the intensity of daylight all around me. I was sleepy, I was groggy, almost dizzy from lack of sleep.

I had known sleep deprivation was a big part of the Safari. That said, it's one thing to register that academically, it's another thing entirely to actually have to push through it. There are two schools of thought on preparing for the sleep deprivation in this race. Some people actually start to wean from sleep in the nights leading up to the race, ostensibly to grow accustomed to operating on less and less sleep. Others advocate sleeping as much as possible the week before the race. I opted for the latter camp, but given that I'm not the best sleeper under regular circumstances, I didn't exactly bank many hours worth note.

This was hard. I was starting to bob and nod off. I shook my head to wake myself up.

*Did I not go to college? Wasn't I the queen of the all-nighter?*

The section between Gonzales and Hochheim (pronounced hoe-hime) is 38 miles, one of the longest distances in the race between any two checkpoints. It's recommended that racers travel with extra water in this section. There are no public access points, no dams, no portages, no logjams, no recreational areas, no bridges. There was nothing from Gonzales to Hochheim except the sound of the word "hut" over and over like a low, constant drumbeat. That, and a lot of sunshine. Too much sunshine.

Since we were back to daylight hours, I added the Cytomax electrolyte powder back into my water jug. I sucked on my drink tube thinking how awful it was to already be this hot at 7:30 in the morning. Hygiene wasn't my concern, as evidenced by the mud and grime covering my shirt and tights. Phil was 24 feet away so I doubt he could smell me. My chief concern was my own personal misery. It was just plain wrong to have stinging sweat dripping into my eyes before eight o'clock in the morning.

For an hour or so we were seeing other racers, some were paddling hard, others were just rousing from their napping spots on gravel bars. We passed a solo racer named Zoltan whom Phil knew.

"Hey man, how's it going?"

Zoltan sounded jolly, "Good! Good!" He seemed like he was doing well, paddling at a leisurely pace. Unfortunately Zoltan would later suffer a hernia and would have to quit the race at the Cheapside Checkpoint.

Once my eyes adjusted to the harshness of the sun and we settled into a rhythmic paddling clip, my mind started to wander. I was intrigued to be paddling the Guadalupe by the light of day. As a kid, I spent every summer at my great-grandmother's river house at

Banning Collins and Christine Warren at the TWS Prelim Race in April 2010

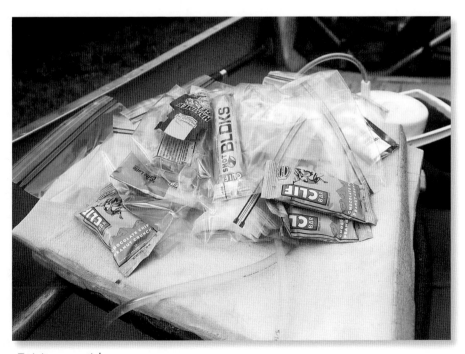

Training essentials

Above: Banning ponders the portage at Cummings Dam

Below: Banning, Christine, and Tom Warren on race day: July 10, 2010

Phil Meyer and Christine rigging their boat

The ready area at Aquarena Springs

At the starting line: final instructions and well-wishes from emcee Tom Goynes

Shotgun start at the headwaters of the San Marcos River

Phil and Christine starting the race in last place

Chaos at Rio Vista Rapids

The Hippie Chicks: Debbie Richardson, Janie Glos and Ginsie Stauss
(photo by Christopher Jacob)

Spectators cooling off on race day

Team Paddlefish near Cottonseed Rapid

Opposite: The stairway portage at Staples Dam

Above: Race official updating the checkpoint sheets

Team captain Monica Harmon with Phil and Christine below Staples Dam

Monica getting a hand from Duck Johnston at the Luling Checkpoint

The Marines in their six-man aluminum boat

Headlamps and mosquitoes at the Palmetto Checkpoint

Duck and Monica restocking ice socks at Cheapside

Above: Sophie and Duck preparing clean water jugs

Opposite: Monica discussing the next leg with Phil and Christine

Mile marker 160 at Cuero: 10:30 pm on Sunday, July 11

Above: Slogging through the muck near Victoria

Opposite: Arriving at the Saltwater Barrier, 16 miles to go

Above: Christine and Phil reviewing a map of Guadalupe Bay

Opposite: Team Paddlefish leaving the Saltwater Barrier

Above: The finish line at the City Park Pavilion in Seadrift, TX

Opposite: Sophie and Duck celebrating Team Paddlefish's arrival

Nearing the seawall

Above: Climbing the steps 10:21 AM on Tuesday, July 13, 2010

Opposite: Sophie congratulating her mom

Opposite: Sophie, Christine and Tom
Above: Nancy Johnston, Tom Warren, Phil Meyer, Monica Harmon, Christine Warren, Sophie Johnson, Duck Johnston, Tim Cole

| 33 | 167 | 7:05 | | | DANIEL ○ DANIE |  |
|---|---|---|---|---|---|---|
| 34 | 1969 | 7:29 | | Tue | HIPPY CHICKS ☺ |  |
| 35 | 746 | 07:42 | | | Taylor/Park |  |
| 36 | 1620 | 07:42:04 | | | Moss/Jacobs |  |
| 37 | 424 | 9:40 | | Tue | Weber X3 |  |
| 38 | 77 | 9:45 | | " | Kent Harlan |  |
| 0 | 324 | 9:50 | | Tues | Max + Mike | Sx |
| 0 | 5311 | 10:21 | | TUES | Team PADDLEfish |  |
| 4 |  |  |  |  |  |  |
| ? |  |  |  |  |  |  |
| 3 |  |  |  |  |  |  |

The final checkpoint sheet: 73 hours, 21 minutes

The coveted Texas Water Safari patch

Hunt, Texas, near the spring-fed headwaters. I learned to swim there, as did my mother, my grandmother, and my great-grandmother. Her house was well above the confluence where the San Marcos flows into the Guadalupe, and above the Safari race route, but it was still nostalgic. I'd been in love with this river my whole life.

I liked the fact that both of these rivers in the Safari bubbled up right here in Texas. We were riding 100% home-brewed water all the way to the coast.

At this spot the Guadalupe appeared so different than it did up in the Hill Country near its origin. It was hard to reconcile that yesterday we had covered the entire San Marcos with its clear waters, narrow hairpin turns, and trees jutting out at us from every angle and every bank. By contrast, this part of the Guadalupe was wide, slow and muddy. There were scattered gravel bars, but most of the banks were tall and steep.

Racers have always complained about this stretch. No one likes the grind to Hochheim. It's a long, slow 38 miles with nothing to get your adrenalin going, nothing to portage, nothing to force you from your seat. No exciting rapids worth mentioning. The mind game portion of the race had officially begun.

About 9:15 a.m. we reached a landmark called Hell's Gate, a spot marked by a towering rock wall that reminded me of something you'd see in a 1960s Western; Indians on horseback, high on the cliff, looking down at the settlers intruding on their lands.

After the rock wall, the river stretched out with a set of rapids that seems uncharacteristic for this area. Unlike the treacherous rapids we'd conquered the day before with large rocks, stumps, twists and turns, this looked more like a giant riffle that you might find on a Rocky Mountain river. Frankly, it looked like perfect trout water.

Our speed picked up a bit through the riffle, but otherwise we paddled by Hell's Gate without consequence. I started to realize it had been a long time since we'd seen anyone else.

"Where are the other racers? We haven't seen anyone else in awhile."

"Everybody is spreading out…hut."

At around 10 a.m. it became stifling hot with no breeze and Phil announced his need for a swim.

"Great idea I'm dying."

We couldn't find a gravel bar but pulled off into a small cove that was slightly shaded. The water felt good but the bottom was really soft and I immediately sank up to my knees. While I enjoyed the chance to cool off and have a pee break, I was worried about expending the energy to hoist my legs out of the muck, or losing a shoe in the thick clingy mud.

We chatted lightly and sang our way through the next couple of hours. We belted out the new Team Paddlefish classics, including the Eagles and Don McLean favorites that had carried us through the previous night on our rough trek to the Gonzales Dam. Sadly no one was around to hear our harmonizing. There were 94 boats in this race but we couldn't buy an audience. The river was utterly empty; no racers, no local residents, no fisherman, no race officials, no one.

Of course, because it was hot as a kiln out on the river, they were probably all indoors enjoying the greatest invention in the history of mankind: air-conditioning.

Oddly, I began to long for the throngs of spectators from the day before with their annoying horns and cowbells. I missed the encouraging homemade signs and the total strangers screaming "Go Team Paddlefish!" as we passed them and they read the side of our boat. It was so chaotic yesterday on the San Marcos I needed a breather, but now I could use a little bank-side boost. Be careful what you wish for, I suppose.

"Phil, I hate to say it but I have to take another dip."

He steered us to another muddy bank where we could get out. The water was about the same temperature as a warm bathtub, but I didn't care. It was infinitely cooler than paddling down the middle of the river without a lick of shade. Plus it felt good on my muscles and joints to be out of the boat and floating for a second.

These breaks never seemed long enough. But we were worried they were adding up and slowing us down. Without any landmarks or dams or bridges it was hard to mark our progress. Everything looked the same. Were we on track to get to Hochheim at a decent pace? Who knew? It felt like we were paddling in oatmeal.

Back into the boat, back to paddling.

At around noon I remarked to Phil that we were probably getting close to a mid-river gravel bar called Monkey Island. Either Phil wasn't too concerned about this upcoming landmark or he didn't hear me correctly because our conversation immediately derailed.

"Monkey butt is the worst," Phil proclaimed.

In last year's race he apparently suffered a violent case of diaper rash. Somehow, for reasons that are unclear to me, a photograph of his bare and flaming rear end found its way to the internet, and despite the fact that I'm fairly certain he was the one that posted the photo, he now lives in mortal fear of getting the monkey butt again. To prevent that ailment he slathered himself in copious amounts of Desitin before the race, and again at the Gonzales Checkpoint. Desitin was soaking through his tights and into the foam on his seat, and I swear there was a white cloud around him in the water on one of our dips. Phil was heavy-handed with the Desitin, but so far he had avoided the dreaded monkey butt.

I laughed out loud thinking of the little red-ass monkeys I'd seen in Africa. Those nasty baboons lurked around our hunting camp when I was in Zimbabwe back in 1989. I had just graduated from high school and was there on safari with my parents. The word "safari" comes from the Swahili term for "safar" which means "journey". The etymological link between my African safari and this race is evident, but so are the differences. Namely, Africa wasn't *nearly* this hot.

At around 1:00 p.m. we rounded a bend and saw actual real people standing up high on the right bank.

"Looks like they're wearing orange hats," Phil remarked.

Our Team Paddlefish hats were orange with our logo and everyone on our chase team had been wearing them throughout the race. My heart soared. Was I going to get a glimpse of my family? How had they found their way up there? Were we that close to Hochheim? I thought we had a ways to go. This was promising.

I sat up straight and paddled with my eyes on those people. There were three of them. Where did they come from? I didn't see a house or a building anywhere in sight. There wasn't a car. No spectator chairs. Just three people standing there on the edge of a high cliff overlooking the river.

My heart sank as we paddled into view. Not my family. Not Tom. Not my mom or dad or Sophie. Just some random strangers. I no longer cared to speculate who they were or how they got there.

We paddled by and sort of nodded up at them. They seemed equally disappointed; I guess we weren't the team they were looking for, either.

I was determined not to ask for another swim break. I was wilting in the heat and knew the water would feel good, but I was also sick to death of paddling this leg of the race and wanted it to be done. I was desperate to get to Hochheim and could think of little else. I tried like hell to daydream about anything that would get my mind off the warm, soporific effects of the sun.

It must have been about 1:30 p.m. when Phil suggested we pull over and take a nap, but I didn't want to stop. We may have had the momentum of sludge at that point, but I just couldn't bear to break our stride no matter how lava-like it was.

"Phil, listen, we are so close. Maybe just an hour or so away. It will be such a morale boost to see our team. Let's just push on and then we can nap right after Hochheim. I really think we need to get that checkpoint behind us."

He didn't react.

"How about I steer for awhile and you can have a break?"

"All right."

Fueled by my new leadership role I pointed at a gravel bar. "Pull over there. We'll get a quick dip to wake us up and we can switch spots."

I settled into Phil's Desitin soaked seat in the stern and began to steer the boat. Soon we both fell into some sort of half-life trance. I was glad to have the responsibility of steering, it gave me something to focus on. But it was a lot harder than in training, with much more pressure. I was careful to pick the fastest seams, leveraging the speediest places in the river. I focused on the nuances of the pedals and tried not to over-steer. There weren't many obstacles down here, nothing like the San Marcos, but there were still a few boils, eddies and small trees that seemed ever-ready to trip me up.

The view from the back of the boat was a refreshing change. Everything seemed so much more open in the back. After staring at the bow of the boat for so long, it was curious to have this vantage point, a clear view of everything we were ferrying down river.

While my feet and shoes and muddy tights weren't terribly entertaining to look at, I did note how much different my legs appeared, now, than they did ten months ago when the serious training started. There was tone and definition that I hadn't seen before. It's odd how goals and perspectives change when life's milestones begin to inch closer. My fortieth birthday was coming, and I was in the best physical shape of my life, with a beautiful daughter, a loving boyfriend, a great family, and a huge support network pushing me down this river. Training and dieting have taken some of the typical dread out of the big four-zero number.

Looking back, though, it wasn't that long ago when my outlook was considerably less buoyant.

———

In September of 2005 I was freshly divorced, clinging to fleeting laughs and short spurts of fun here and there to get me through the dark funk. On the morning of my 35th birthday, I bought a fabulous new pair of smoking-hot designer jeans that needed to be hemmed in time for my party, that night. The alteration shop said they couldn't do a same-day order, so I threw myself at the mercy of the owner. I cooed and apologized and begged and sweet-talked. I explained how I was recently divorced and this was my first birthday celebration as a single girl and I just had to look fabulous at the party. Finally she agreed to have them ready for me later that afternoon.

At 5:00 p.m. I jumped in the car to retrieve my jeans without considering my attire. I was sporting black leggings smeared with dried paint, and a ratty, oversized t-shirt that I grabbed from the pile of unwanted clothes my ex-husband left behind. I looked pretty gamey, but I figured I would shower after I ran errands.

The alterations shop was chaos. A team of bridesmaids was wreaking havoc on the place. Businessmen were impatiently flicking their claim tickets. One particularly handsome guy was being fitted for a tuxedo. The Owner Maven was holed up in the back room and her Worker Bee was not on top of things. I waited and waited and waited. Suddenly from across the room, the Worker Bee barked directly at me and asked what I needed. I answered over everyone's heads that I was picking up jeans that were a same-day rush. She pointed at me and replied loudly, "Oh yeah! The maternity jeans?"

Time stopped. Chatter ceased. The air left the room. Everyone turned and stared at me. They sized me up, head to toe, to see if was indeed pregnant. I knew I looked grungy in my giant t-shirt, but horror of horrors—did I look fat? At this point I had a choice; I could correct the Worker Bee (and make her feel awful) because I was not there to pick up maternity jeans. Or I could revert back to my sweet southern upbringing and also save face with the bitchy bridesmaids and the hot tuxedo guy who were all staring, waiting to see how this would play out.

I smiled as sweetly as I could and said, "Yes! I'm here for the maternity jeans! Are they ready?"

The Worker Bee bagged up the gigantic pants of some absentee pregnant woman and I carried them out the door as fast as I could (without endangering my faux baby, of course). Figuring that it would take at least twenty minutes for their clientele to turn over, I drove the maternity pants around the neighborhood like a (non-pregnant) lunatic, and then returned them to the shop for my own. Thank God, the Worker Bee was busy in the back and the Owner Maven was able to handle the exchange without further embarrassment.

Getting fit has been an on again off again struggle in my life, always looming and never far from my mind. I'm no different than many women. Basically I've been trying to lose the same 15-20 pounds since the sixth grade when I bought the book, "Thin Thighs in 30 Days," an early eighties fitness sensation. It's laughable to think that I was focused on my figure when I was that young, but woefully I will admit, that's when the struggle began.

Over time I developed a rather Faustian relationship with diet and exercise. I'd go through phases where I walked a little here, walked a little there, all the while indulging in burgers and queso and knowing full well that when I hit a certain point all I would have to do is amp up the workouts, reduce the carbs, and presto! I'd be right back in my cute closet.

For the most part that plan worked pretty well, but there were some years when I couldn't seem to win the battle of the burger. In my mid-thirties, around the time of the maternity jeans incident, I decided it was time to shed some real weight, so in my own version of portion control I simply started ordering the Kid's Meal at Whataburger and was actually able to trim a few (temporary) pounds.

Having researched and tried my hand at almost every fad diet that has come down the pipeline, I ultimately dove into the South Beach Diet. Starting right after my 36th birthday, I eliminated all simple carbs from my life. The results were good on the scale, but as with all deals that stem from shallow, self-focused motives, there comes a time when you have to pay up. Apparently the pounds I lost on South Beach had a built-in homing device because they found their way back to me, *pronto*—and they were pissed! They returned extra clingy and needy, making my life a living hell.

The Water Safari came along at the perfect time. It was a goal-driven structured way to retool my eating and my exercise regime. I knew it was time to tackle my nutrition and training from the vantage point of genuine health, not vanity. I needed to be inspired by how things were working inside, not how I was going to fit into a pair of white jeans better than I had last summer.

When I asked people for their advice about my diet and nutrition, some said to eat lots of pasta, but I couldn't wrap my head around that. I mean, the race was ten months away, and at that point I just needed to lose weight. Piles of pasta energy didn't seem necessary at that stage, and I already knew that the South Beach Diet wouldn't work, so I decided to poll a bigger populace.

After a couple of posts about dieting and nutrition on my blog, *Fly Fish Chick*, I caught the attention of an angel of a woman, Melissa Jory, a sports nutritionist in Boulder, Colorado. As a contribution to the Team Paddlefish charitable cause, she decided to donate her time and professional services to counsel me on my nutrition… or lack thereof.

First off: Melissa wanted to start me on a three-week cleanse. A strict healthy diet; like *real* healthy. We set a practical date to start the cleanse, Monday September 14, my 39th birthday.

Like a death row inmate ordering a last meal, I went wild on the day before my birthday and indulged in a total blowout that started with a massive Mexican brunch. From there, my girlfriends and I spent the afternoon at Ginny's Little Longhorn, a legendary honky tonk where Dale Watson plays every Sunday afternoon for Chicken Shit Bingo. It's an Austin classic. You buy a ticket with a handwritten number on it. They put a chicken in a cage that has bingo numbers all over the bottom. If the chicken poops on your number, you win the pot of cash.

Unfortunately, Ginny's original bingo chicken had been killed by a raccoon a day or so before our gluttony fest, so they were using a loaner. It had to be an omen that drastic change was imminent when the new chicken, performing right next to Ginny's Crock-pot Chili Dog Buffet, was named "Tofu."

The next morning I awoke and opened my refrigerator that was packed with things I never imagined that I'd buy.

*Goat kefir? Are you serious? What part of the goat does THAT come from?*

I kicked off Melissa's cleanse with one of her Hemp-Chia Breakfast Smoothies.

For the next few weeks I ate organic fruits and vegetables, organic pasteurized eggs, organic chicken apple sausage, dark leafy green salads with homemade dressing, raw almond butter and flax seed crackers, organic brown rice and quinoa, and limited (goat) dairy. No caffeine, sugar, alcohol, processed or packaged foods, or wheat.

Melissa explained the rationale behind choosing organic. Basically, every single ounce of energy in my body during training should be spent on paddling, on sweating properly, on staying cool, on staying hydrated, on not cramping. I would be asking a lot from my organs and it wasn't fair to add preservatives and chemicals to their to-do list.

The three week cleanse went pretty well. I lost 4.5 pounds, which was a big morale boost. I wanted to lose so much that friends and family would be instantly worried I was too thin. But that didn't happen, and Melissa counseled me to be more responsible.

Eliminating sugar helped my back pain immensely. Sugar is a known inflammatory which is aggravating to disks and nerves that are already inflamed. Melissa also had me taking fish oil supplements as another anti-inflammatory strategy. On the label of that bottle was a clever marketing lever that said "Controls Fish Burps."

Good to know.

As the three week cleanse drew toward an end, Melissa sent me my nutrition plan for the next nine months of training. But the long term eating plan sounded a lot like the cleanse. Like Tofu the chicken, I was beginning to suspect I was part of a bigger game plan. It seemed that the cleanse was a classic bait and switch.

Even though Melissa didn't actually use that term, she did explain that the cleanse was never meant to be a quick-fix, three-week absolution for all my eating sins. This was an awakening to a whole new relationship with food, a new way of eating, a new way of living. Living whole and holy living.

I did a pretty good job throughout the fall, winter, and spring, all things considered. I indulged here and there, but I kept eating the Hemp-Chia Smoothies which changed my complexion and digestive tract for the better. I limited my meals to lean white meats, adding more vegetables than ever before. I drank red wine and hardly any beer or liquor. I avoided wheat products as best as I could. I chose organic when the budget allowed.

When I started talking with people about how to physically train for the race, I found a broad pool of advice. Running, which I despised; swimming, which I loved and was easy on my back; Pilates, which would help my core; the rowing machine, which made sense.

Everyone had an opinion, but the Safari veterans all trumpeted the same command: paddling.

Banning and I made weekly paddling runs in the fall, but the serious river miles didn't come until after the first of the year. By

March we were on a consistent schedule that involved two small paddle runs (10-15 miles) and one long run (25-40 miles) every week, plus a regular cardio and weight workout about three times a week.

That routine typically started with 90 minutes on the rowing machine, followed by 30 minutes of treadmill, 30 minutes on the elliptical, an hour of weight training, and 30 minutes of Pilates floor mat work. It was a punishing grind, but I kept it up by celebrating my small victories, most notable of which was my eventual running pace of three miles in 30 minutes. During the months leading up to the Safari I would frequently ask myself, "What can I do *right this very second* to reach my goal? What can I do *right this very second* to reach Seadrift? What can I do *right this very second* to get a patch?"

The answer was clear on days we paddled: paddle well, learn the portages and don't break the boat. It was also pretty clear when I was in the gym: do the machines longer and faster. But the more I started asking myself those questions, the more curious the answers became. If I was at my desk working, I'd stand and stretch regularly. If I started getting bored with the machines at the gym, I'd spend a few dollars on iTunes and buy new songs for my workout playlists. If I was in the kitchen I'd choose something healthy and fresh from the refrigerator as opposed to something packaged from the pantry. If I was on an airplane on my way to visit Tom, I would pull out the mileage charts and memorize the checkpoints and key obstacles along the river. If I was in my car, waiting for Sophie to come out of school, I'd sit up straight, engage my abs and improve my posture. Sometimes what I really needed more than exercise was to turn off the computer and TV and rest for an hour.

I was surprised by my newfound self-discipline. When Tom and I went to a three-day music festival, camping with friends, he helped me make a giant batch of Melissa's smoothies and other healthy treats for the weekend. When I went to the Bahamas on a bonefish trip with Sophie and my parents, I woke up every morning, snuck into the teeny bathroom at the condo and did pushups, sit-ups, planks, Pilates, and jumping jacks.

While my diet and exercise transitions were by no means an overnight success, by the time race day came around I was strong, toned, healthy and weighed considerably less than when I bought my ticket at Chicken Shit Bingo back in September.

———

At around 1:30, the muffled sounds of traffic snapped me out of my daydreaming.

"Phil, do you hear cars?"

"Yeah. Yeah I do."

"You know what cars mean?"

"Yep."

"Cars mean bridges and the next bridge is Hochheim!"

We pulled over and switched places so Phil could guide us in. But we weren't as close as we thought, and the river kept turning and bending with no bridge in sight. For another half hour we paddled and paddled. I was becoming convinced that the name Hochheim was a fancy derivative of ho-hum because this was the most boring stretch of river on the planet.

As desolate as this part of the river seemed, it enjoyed some mildly interesting history. It is said that the very first European encounter ever on the Guadalupe happened right here at the present day site of Hochheim. Around 1528 Álvar Núñez Cabeza de Vaca, a Spanish explorer, arrived at the river right in this area and nick-named the Guadalupe "The River of Nuts." They say he was inspired by the abundance of pecan trees on the banks, but clearly he was clairvoyant and having premonitions of lycra-clad paddlers baking their brains in the mid-summer heat.

The town Hochheim was named for Volentine Hoch, a German immigrant who arrived in 1848 and built a stone home up high on the banks of the river. Translated, Hochheim actually means "high home." The house became the hub of trading and commerce activity as Hochheim was on the stage coach route from Austin to the coast. Once a bustling hotspot, by the 1980's Hochheim's population dwindled to about 70 people with only one business remaining.

When we rounded the next bend, the checkpoint bridge finally came into view. I was ecstatic and couldn't wait to see everyone, especially since Sophie and my mom were still at their motel when we came through Gonzales.

Phil steered us toward the right bank under the bridge. I was glad he was back on the pedals because it was a little tricky to angle into the checkpoint. We had to thread the needle between bridge pilings on our left, which stand in the middle of the river, and a concrete pad river right on the bank beneath the bridge. I felt like we were wheeling into a driveway of sorts and smiled at our chase team as they cheered from the concrete pad.

Hochheim was a crummy, nasty checkpoint. Our team looked like trolls living under a bridge, but I was thrilled to see them and euphoric to have this stretch behind me. As we pulled into the chute I laughed and shouted to our team, "Can I get a Whataburger with cheese?"

I couldn't help myself. It just felt like we were cruising up to a drive-through window. I thought it was funny. Phil did not.

"Hey!" he shouted at me. "Pay attention!"

BAM! We smashed the bow into a concrete piling.

He was flustered and I think fairly humiliated in front of the large crowd that hovered up at the top of the hill. I was somewhat embarrassed but also thought he needed to lighten up. I was going to savor the nanoseconds we had at this checkpoint. I was so happy to see everyone.

We dumped our trash and traded out fresh water jugs while my dad and Tom cheered for us. Monica was as sweet and organized as ever. Phil was all business. Tim Cole was shooting photos. I was chatting with our support team while I mixed Cytomax into my water and placed new ice socks on my neck and on my lower back. I wondered if we needed to check the bow of the boat but figured that Phil didn't want to assess the damage in front of everyone at the checkpoint.

Tom was fired up as he shared, "Banning's been calling from his trip. He says tons of people are rooting for y'all on Facebook and on your blog. The comments are pouring in. People are cheering for Team Paddlefish!" I smiled at that message and looked up at Sophie and my mom up on the bank.

Cliff swallow nests lined the underbelly of the bridge, hanging down like stalactites in a cave. The whole place reeked of mud, bird dung, and decay, but as bad as it smelled, I really didn't want to paddle out from the shade back into the sunshine. I didn't want to leave my family. Mere minutes were not enough.

But it was time to press on. We were barely out of earshot from our chase team when Phil launched into a diatribe about crashing into the bridge piling. I couldn't take it. I snapped. Blame it on the heat, blame it on lack of sleep, but this sweet-to-a-point southern belle popped her claws and prepared to scratch back.

Phil and I were about to have a good old-fashioned quarrel.

## Hochheim Checkpoint

| | |
|---|---|
| CUTOFF TIME: | MONDAY 10:00 A.M. |
| OUR TIME: | SUNDAY 2:04 P.M. |
| PLACE: | 48TH |
| TIME ELAPSED: | 29 HOURS AND 4 MINUTES |
| MILES PADDLED: | 123 |
| MILES TO GO: | 137 |

# CHAPTER 18

# HOCHHEIM TO CHEAPSIDE

*"If you understood everything I said, you'd be me."*
–Miles Davis

It was bound to happen. Every Safari veteran that I had talked to in the year leading up to this race had emphatically told me that teammate squabbles were inevitable in such intimate and extreme conditions, and as we pulled away from the Hochheim Checkpoint, our number was up.

Basically Phil was angry that we crashed into the bridge piling. His main beef was that Tom and my dad were talking to me too much at the checkpoints and distracting me and that's why we hit the concrete piling.

I was willing to go down this path. "Phil, did you call a hut that I didn't do? Did you call a draw stroke that I didn't do? I didn't hear you call out either."

"There's just too much going on at the checkpoints."

"I get that you don't like the activity at the checkpoints. That's clear. And I trust you that we need to be quick, in and out, so we don't sink a lot of time there. But I am one half of this team and I need to see my family at the checkpoints. Certainly you can see that the whole of Team Paddlefish benefits if I get a quick morale boost at the checkpoints talking with my family?"

"We don't have the luxury of wrecking this boat."

"I get that, Phil. But I don't think our hitting the piling is linked to the checkpoints. We could have hit a stump miles down-river with no one around. You just don't like the checkpoints and the fact that I like to interact, there, with my family."

"I don't like that Tom was talking so much that he wrecked our boat."

In a flash my face got so hot it felt like the sun had lurched about a few million miles closer to us. "Are you out of your *mind*?"

"He shouldn't have been—"

"No. I am going to stop you right there. You *do not* get to talk about him. It is insane that you are going to blame him for wrecking our boat. It's *our* boat, Phil. We are the only two in it. I was the one laughing and talking silly, and frankly, you were the one steering. How in the hell could *he* wreck our boat?"

"He's distracting you."

"He's not *distracting* me, Phil. Honestly I think this is some-thing you might want to take a look at in your life. Seriously. I mean if you are capable in your mind of actually believing that he wrecked our boat? I think you place too much blame on other people. It's always someone else's fault. There is a serious perception-reality gap here."

We went round and round as these debased arguments tend to do. We only paddled about 45 minutes away from Hochheim be-fore we stopped for a nap around 3 p.m. We pulled the boat onto a gravel bar and walked into some tall trees for shade. Despite how angry and annoyed I was, I fell asleep remarkably quickly.

I probably napped about twenty minutes. Phil was up walk-ing around and messing with the boat. I kept my eyes closed and pre-tended to sleep for another ten minutes or so. I wasn't very comfortable but I wasn't ready to leave the shade and venture back to the sunlight.

Guilt and obligation got the best of me. I knew we should press on. So I roused from my rocky dirt bed and put my hat and shoes back on. I was so freaking tired. My body was numb and well past the point of exhaustion. I stretched to get the blood flowing.

I walked over to Phil and the boat. The sun was searing so I took the opportunity to submerge for a minute before we left. I decided I needed to close the book on my portion of the argument and was ready to extend an olive branch.

"Phil, listen. I'm sorry I was talking when we were paddling into Hochheim. If I missed a draw stroke because of it, I wasn't aware. I am sorry about the boat."

"The boat's not that bad. I put some duct tape on it. Just a small tear. We should be fine. We just can't afford to do it again."

I was relieved the boat was okay but found it interesting that he didn't feel the need to apologize or take even an ounce of responsibility. I shooed those immature thoughts from my mind. My apology was not conditional, as apologies shouldn't be. It was an apology, I meant it, I gave it. It shouldn't hinge on his contrition or lack thereof.

*Right?*

*Yes.*

*Move on.*

We paddled on talking lightly or not at all. The afternoon was hot. The temperature was well above 100 degrees. Where was the breeze? It almost made me want to paddle faster just to create a little breeze on my face.

At around 4 p.m. we stopped for a quick drink/snack/swim/ pee break and Phil brought up our argument, "It's really common to have a fight about this place during the Safari. We are almost halfway done. Teams always argue on day two."

"It makes sense. The heat and the pressure."

"I just hope everything is okay. I mean it's not that big of a thing."

"No! Not at all. Phil, I am all about getting it all out and moving on. We need to move on."

"I agree. I like to just let things go."

I was pleasantly surprised we were reaching this mature point relatively soon. This seemed like genuine progress. Until it wasn't.

Phil added, "I think I am going to give your family a speech at the next checkpoint about how they wrecked our boat and how they need to be more quiet and not distract you."

The surge of rage I felt in my body probably rocked the boat. I can't believe I didn't capsize us when I fired back, "Over my dead body. Are you out of your mind? There is no way in hell you are going to speak to my dad or my boyfriend like that. You are not going to give them some condescending speech—"

"They just need to know—"

"Listen Phil. They don't *need* to know anything. They don't even *need* to be here. They have gone to great expense, exhaustion and inconvenience to help us with this race. They are *helping* our team captain. They are rooting for *you*. They don't *need* to do a *damn* thing."

"I'm just gonna lay it out for them."

"I swear on my life if you attempt to say one word I will tell them to leave. I'll tell them to just meet me in Seadrift. I will tell them not to lift one more finger for Team Paddlefish."

"I'm not trying to start the fight again. I am all about putting that behind us."

"Well this is very much not putting it behind us. Do you understand these are grown men? They don't need you reprimanding them like they're in kindergarten. My dad would feel so bad if he thought he did *anything* to detract from our success. Which he hasn't. And I am not letting you speak like that to my boyfriend. Period."

"I just think they need to know they put a hole in the boat."

"Phil, *you* were steering the boat! *You* were on the pedals. Stop! Just stop. Stop and think about how ridiculous you sound. I get that I might have missed a stroke. I take full responsibility for making the jokey comment on the way in. Perhaps I distracted you. It was either you, or it was me, or it was a combination—but it was someone in *this* boat. *Our* boat. The one we are paddling and steering all by ourselves. Leave them out of it."

I was incensed.

I doubted my point was getting through but at least we paddled in silence for awhile.

Until…

He started again. "I just think at the next checkpoint I am going to tell them—"

"Phil, stop. Just stop talking about this. It's not going to happen. I will do it. I will say something to them. But honestly, I swear on my life, if you open your mouth to speak to my dad or Tom I will send them to Seadrift to wait this out and Monica will have to team captain this deal alone. And I will be livid."

"I'm not trying to bring this argument back up."

"Oh my gosh! Are you *freaking* kidding me? This is the very definition of bringing it back up. Just quit. Quit. Let it go."

"I want to let it go."

"Well then actually let it go. Just stop talking about it. Jeez, you have issues."

Phil glanced down at the GPS mounted on the cross bar in front of him. "Man, every time I bring this up you start paddling a lot faster. Maybe I should keep pissing you off and we'll get to Seadrift sooner."

Okay, that was pretty funny. Nothing like a touch of humor to eddy out of a ridiculously inane case of locked horns.

"Phil, I will be the one to talk to the team at the next checkpoint. Don't bring it up again. If you want me to paddle faster just say so."

It was probably 4:30 or 5 p.m. when we paddled across the

halfway mark. 130 miles and we were halfway there. Quite an accomplishment. Again, I should have been more exuberant. But I felt half victorious, half deflated. I was excited that the treachery of the San Marcos was behind us, but knew we still had the giant logjam and the bay ahead of us. I was half awake, half asleep. I couldn't tell if the glass was half empty or half full.

Then again, with each stroke there was less mileage ahead of us than behind us. That felt halfway good.

At some point we caught up with Sam Hilker, a twenty-something young woman who was paddling Women's Solo. Sam had made quite a name for herself as a solo racer, and aside from being an incredible athlete, she was exceptionally sweet and cool. Sam's fiancé, Wade Binion, was paddling on a six-man team that was in contention to win the Safari.

It was a blessing to run into her at this point on the river, and it was good for Phil and me to have some company. Phil knew Sam so they chatted quite a bit while I enjoyed paddling in silence. I chimed in here and there. Sam was a double-blade paddler, by nature, but in the midst of our conversation, she put away her two-bladed paddle, popped a few ibuprofen, and deployed her single blade paddle. "My shoulders are killing me," she shared.

Phil had explained to me early on in our training the pros and cons of doubles and singles. "Double-blading is a lot faster. It's a no brainer in shorter races. But it requires super accurate form to reduce the wear and tear on your muscles. It really takes a toll on your shoulders in a race this long."

He turned back to Sam, "Have you heard anything about the logjam down there below Dupont?"

Sam was low-key as she replied, "Yeah, it's still there. It's basically broken up into three logjams now."

"Three? How bad?"

"Well I haven't seen it. Wade just went down last week and

trained it. So his info is pretty fresh. Basically he told me how to deal with it. Just as soon as you reach the first logjam, veer right and take the cut into Alligator Lake. Keep along the left bank of Alligator Lake. Stay along the left the whole time to keep you oriented so you don't get lost in the lake. When that ends, you pop back into the main river and you just have to portage the last logjam which isn't supposed to be that bad."

"So he's telling you to go *into* Alligator Lake?"

Alligator Lake is the stuff Safari legends are made of. It's not really a lake, per se, with water skiers and swimming areas; it's more like a lowland marsh where the river wanders during high water times and floods a huge shallow basin. There are a number of cuts into Alligator Lake from the main river channel and the entire area is notorious for gobbling up Safari teams, swirling them around past the point of confusion, and disorienting them for hours on end.

There is no two-way communication allowed in the Safari. No CB radios, no walkie-talkies, no cell phones. The only exception in the history of the race was given to a paddler that was required to have a cell phone so he could check in with his parole officer.

At any rate, for emergencies many people do bring a cell phone in a sealed baggie that can be opened once and not resealed. Of course if you open the bag and use the phone you DNF the race, but you might also live. People bring the sealed emergency phones specifically with Alligator Lake in mind.

I was a tad unnerved at the mention of a plan that would take us into Alligator Lake on purpose, but I had complete faith in Phil's call on this one. I hadn't trained the section with the logjam, he'd completed the Safari before. Plus I got the feeling Phil really trusted Sam and her fiancé Wade. They seemed thorough and reliable.

There is so much gamesmanship in the Safari, sometimes it's hard to tell whom to trust. At the Safari orientation they were adamant, "Don't follow a sign that says "Shortcut" unless you put it there yourself." Apparently teams have been known to go down a week or so before the race and try to lead gullible racers off course by posting signs that lead to time-consuming dead-end lakes.

Fortunately, we had some time to talk about how we were going to handle the logjam and Alligator Lake. It was interesting to hear her strategy in the meantime. I wondered if Sam's shoulders were feeling better. I wondered if they could possible hurt as bad as my ass.

I swore to myself then and there I would never again lament the cush on my tush. The layers I was always trying to shed were the only thing saving me at this point. I literally felt like something was drilling into my tailbone. Good lord was I sick of being in that seat. I wanted my fanny out of that canoe so badly. I needed to think about something else. Anything to get my mind off my aching derriere.

Little did I know that some quality free entertainment was on its way.

I started hallucinating somewhere along this stretch to Cheapside. Hallucinations were legendary in Safari lore. I heard about one guy who was seen trying to shove quarters in a tree trunk thinking it was a Coke machine. Another seasoned racer told us about the time he was trying to get his partner to lie down and rest, and his partner replied, "Sure no problem. But first let me just file these papers." One of the scariest hallucinations I'd heard of was more about not seeing something that was actually there. A racer was nearly to the finish line, but he first had to cross the Victoria Barge Canal just before Seadrift. He started paddling across the canal without his eyes and brain registering the massive barge barreling down on him. Another team rushed over and yanked him out of the way with seconds to spare.

My hallucinations started as a misinterpretation of an actual object: a stump that looked like an alligator, a tree trunk that looked like a rowboat. As the day wore on, though, and the combination of heat and sleep deprivation took hold, my mind began to simply conjure up odd visions out of thin air.

On the right side of the river I saw a ski boat near a dock with a group of people lounging and laughing in the sun. I was jealous of their lazy weekend on the river. I wondered if they thought we looked silly in our floppy sun hats and long shirts and tights. As we paddled closer the apparition faded. No people. Not even a dock. Just a tree trunk growing out sideways from the bank.

One of the strangest sights I witnessed was a herd of Jack Russell Terriers on the bank, standing at attention, heads cocked toward the sky, chests puffed out like brave little soldiers waiting for a command.

*What were they waiting for? Who was in charge of them? Wait…where did they go?*

I don't know the science behind hallucinations, nor do I understand why some seem more fleeting than others. The most realistic vision I had on that stagnant and oppressive afternoon was the carcass of a deer impaled on a tree trunk. It was horrifying. Obviously the deer had been washed downriver in the recent flood. It was so crystal clear to me that I actually stopped paddling and spoke out, "How awful for that deer!"

Phil sounded tired and confused, "What?"

We paddled by and suddenly the deer was gone, vaporized like a mirage. There was nothing but a few leafy green twigs hanging on that tree trunk.

"Never mind," I exhaled, thoroughly wiped out. "It's so hot. Are you hot? It is so freaking HOT!"

"It's pretty hot."

Phil seemed disengaged too.

"I think this is the hottest time of day. In Montana, when we're fishing, sometimes it is unbearably hot at about five or six in the evening. Everyone thinks noon is hot. This is hotter."

The sun was getting lower in the sky, but no less hot. In fact, it was now meeting me more at eye level, which was a new brand of torture. As we paddled beside tall trees, the sun would hide and then reappear. The on/off flashing sensation was giving me fits, like Paparazzi camera flashes, or someone flicking the switch on a Q-beam aimed right through my eyes and into my brain.

Phil didn't seem like chatting. My butt hurt so badly I could barely sit still. I had to be careful not to rock the boat, but I started lifting up one cheek at a time trying to relieve the pressure.

Seadrift seemed so far away.

I thought about the naysayers who said I wouldn't finish. I thought about that friend of a friend, Dick Rowe, who said that I didn't have it in me. I thought about how many times I heard the following from otherwise good-natured friends and acquaintances:

1) Yeah, I've heard about the Water Safari…wait…*you* want to do it?
2) You know that's a really hard race, don't you? I mean… it's like *really* hard.
3) A canoe race? Why?

Remembering their jabs seemed to give me a bit of spark. Phil was still quiet in the stern and I began paddling a bit faster.

*Dick Rowe…I simply had to prove that guy wrong…*

Like some half-crazed human metronome, I spent the next half-hour using his name to set my paddle cadence.

*Dick Rowe. Dick Rowe. Dick Rowe. Dick Rowe…*

Eventually I grew tired of the negative energy associated with proving this person wrong, so I started to think of how incredible it was going to feel paddling up to Seadrift, celebrating with my family and hugging Sophie for the first time in over three weeks.

*Seadrift. Seadrift. Seadrift. Seadrift…*

It was close to 6 p.m. when I looked at my watch. Surely we

were getting close. The Cheapside Checkpoint was at the Highway 766 bridge just north of Cuero.

The town of Cuero is known as the Turkey Capital of the World. Their high school mascot is a Fighting Gobbler, and each fall they celebrate their heritage with an annual Turkey Fest. When the town was originally settled and named, turkey was not yet king in Cuero. The word "Cuero" actually means "hide" in Spanish. Cuero was a stopping point on the Chisholm Trail, so hides were traded and a profitable tannery industry flourished.

These days Cuero is best known for its frequency of chupacabra sightings. A chupacabra is a mythical (or real) creature whose name means "goatsucker" in Spanish. Apparently these half coyote, half bear-like beasts with massive fangs and a row of spines running down their backs are known for sucking the blood out of livestock. Not only have several ranchers and citizens in Cuero spotted the chupacabra, they have actually retrieved some dead ones. Of course, DNA tests stated that they were actually just coyotes with mange, but chupacabra enthusiasts worldwide dispute those findings vehemently with their own set of facts.

*I wished I could see a chupacabra. That would certainly trump the bobcat and the swimming hogs. Couldn't I at least hallucinate one?*

When the Cheapside Checkpoint finally came into view, my thoughts returned, again, to our squabble earlier in the day.

Phil was excited, but I curtly reminded him, "Don't bring it up, let me do the talking."

The orange Team Paddlefish hats were a pleasant sight. We pulled in carefully and lodged the boat against the muddy bank. As usual Sophie stayed up top with my mom and waved down. Tom and my dad were right there with Monica to help her make the transfers.

Before anything was going to happen, I was getting my aching butt out of that boat. I stepped out into thigh-deep water and held on to the gunnel.

When the water transfers were complete, I called the meeting to order.

"Hey y'all, we need to have a quick team meeting. We're over halfway done and getting into the serious part of this race. These checkpoints need to be super efficient. It would be great if y'all could cheer us in, but then we need to get quiet and focused on our business. Then you can cheer us back out."

My dad, perceptive as always, asked "Have we done something wrong? Just tell us what we need to do."

I decided to play the full martyr card. "No, y'all have been great, Daddy, we couldn't do this without you. But I got distracted back there at Hochheim. I was joking around, and we hit the bridge. We're tired and just need to stay super focused. Plus we're making good time and need to keep these checkpoints efficient so we can get there!"

The team was fired up. They seemed to get it, and were excited about the idea that we were so far ahead of the cutoff times. The sun was finally easing below the tree tops (god-freaking-speed) and we decided to go ahead and gear the boat again for night travel. Team Paddlefish talked in hushed tones while we worked. We dumped all our trash. I took new water jugs and again chose not to add the Cytomax electrolytes. We zipped away hats and sunglasses, put on headlamps and attached the bow light. We were ready for the next stretch.

Just as instructed, they cheered loudly again as we pulled away from the Cheapside Checkpoint. We didn't know it at the time, but the winning race boat had arrived in Seadrift about four minutes earlier. The Belizean/Texan team had just taken first place. I'm glad I didn't know that yet. I was still too immersed in my own present situation to stretch my mind that far downriver.

Perhaps it wasn't a constructive approach but I felt obliged to point out to Phil how well my team meeting had gone. "See, you don't have to yell at people or blame them. They got the message without any hurt feelings. It's done."

I don't know what he thought about it, but at that point the issue was truly closed for business. We both seemed in good spirits, and thankfully the whole fracas melted away just as the hot, searing sun drifted off to wherever it goes when it clocks out from its day of torturing paddle racers.

## Cheapside Checkpoint

| | |
|---|---|
| CUTOFF TIME: | MONDAY 3:00 P.M. |
| OUR TIME: | SUNDAY 7:44 P.M. |
| PLACE: | 48TH |
| TIME ELAPSED: | 34 HOURS AND 44 MINUTES |
| MILES PADDLED: | 145 |
| MILES TO GO: | 115 |

# CHAPTER 19

# CHEAPSIDE TO CUERO

*"Since everything is in our heads, we had better not lose them."*
–COCO CHANEL

"Phil, are you cold? I am getting kinda chilled."

"Nope, I'm okay."

"After this afternoon's heat, it's hard to believe I could ever be cold again."

"It's your body. It's fatigue."

Even though we had already spent the afternoon conjuring up mirages, the 15-mile stretch between Cheapside and Cuero has been known for years among Safari paddlers as Hallucination Alley. A lot of teams tend to hit this stretch in the middle of the second night when their minds have reached the full-on tipping point.

*Fifteen miles...*

When we first started training last fall, Banning and I would paddle about seven miles on flat easy water and I would be wiped out for hours afterwards. Too tired to cook, Sophie and I ate a lot of pizza during that stretch. And, now, here I am 145 miles into a 260 mile race and totally stoked that our next stretch was only fifteen miles.

Perspective.

Phil asked from the stern, "What do you know about the Cu-ero Dam? I can't remember it at all from last year."

"I don't have any notes on that. I'm blanking on a dam in this section."

"Oh well, I guess we'll know a dam when we see one."

At that point I thought back to the solo racer and the barge that he didn't see coming.

For the next couple of hours we paddled near a few other race teams. Everyone seemed to be in decent spirits, though most were looking ragged and beat. We paddled in a group of about three or four boats off and on. Sam Hilker was back in our mix. We asked about the Cuero Dam and received a variety of reports on how to deal with it. Apparently it's only the remnants of a once-functional dam. You can run most of it but there are some hairpin turns.

There was still light in the sky when we reached the dam. We pulled back and let Sam and the other teams take the lead since they were more confident about their lines. With decent water levels flow-ing through, it turned out to be a cakewalk. We zigzagged through the decrepit stone walls and popped out the other side unscathed. As much as I wanted to get my bottom out of my seat, I was glad we didn't have to portage up and over any concrete walls.

Sam dropped back and it was nice to paddle alongside her for company. Phil peppered her with more questions about the logjam and the cut through Alligator Lake. She explained it in such detail I was starting to picture it as if I'd actually paddled that section before.

I can't remember who pulled away from whom but soon after dark, Phil and I found ourselves racing alone again. I was shivering at this point. I tried to tough it out but I wasn't thinking clearly, and my teeth were practically chattering. I needed another layer of clothing.

"Phil, I am so cold. I can't stand it. I might have to put on my life vest or something. I have to get out of this wet shirt."

"No don't put on your life vest. Don't you have an extra shirt?"

"Yeah, but it's sealed and down in the mesh bag back by you."

We pulled over to deal with my sudden onset of hypothermia. He reached in and the first vacuum-packed clothing item he extracted was his spare long-sleeved shirt.

"Here," he said. "Just use mine."

"Are you sure?"

"Yeah. It's easier than digging further in there. I'm fine, I don't need it."

"Phil, thank you *so* much!"

I stripped off my once-white, funky brownish-gray wet shirt that I had started the race with. Good riddance. His clean dry shirt was a godsend.

"Oh my gosh, thank you so much." I rubbed my arms to get some friction going and move the blood around. "Okay, I am back in the game. Really, thank you."

"No problem."

We paddled several miles without incident. The sleeves on his shirt were too long and would flap down over my wrists while I paddled, but I didn't care. I would deal with that later. I was so happy to have thwarted that bizarre chill.

Unlike the desolate Hochheim stretch, we were now much closer to civilization. We could hear cars in the distance and passed a few river houses, here and there. One house had a huge screened area and a fabulous deck. Lights were on, and someone was grilling and preparing for a fun summer night on the river.

*Damn them.*

I marveled at how petty and unattractive envy could make me.

As we passed the river houses, I began to wonder exactly where we were in relation to Cuero. In preparing for the race I read about a ghost town called Clinton, which had been a small DeWitt Colony settlement roughly five miles southwest of Cuero. That should put it somewhere near this exact part of the river. Clinton was known for two things: The Sutton-Taylor Feud and Matilda Lockhart.

The Sutton-Taylor Feud was the longest and bloodiest in Texas. The origin of their bickering is unclear; some speculate that the families brought their issues to Texas from states back east, although there is no evidence to support this theory. Violence peaked in the late 1860s after the Civil War. Reconstruction was a time for complete chaos and vigilante law in this area. The Sutton and Taylor families spent over a decade avenging deaths, escaping prison, and hunting each other down. Gun fights the likes of which inspired Western movies played out for real in the saloon and streets of Clinton. In the end, the Suttons lost 13 lives and the Taylors lost 22.

It's hard to have too much sympathy for a couple of lunatic families bent on killing each other, but it is humanly impossible not to feel horror and outrage at what happened to poor Matilda Lockhart.

She was 13 years old in 1838. Her family had come to Texas from Illinois and settled on the Guadalupe River near Clinton. One day Matilda, her sister, and some other children were picking pecans on the riverbank in this same stretch that we were paddling. When they were spotted by Comanches that had wandered into southeast Texas on another plundering raid, Matilda ran and would have likely escaped if one of the younger girls hadn't begged her not to leave her behind. Matilda, her sister, and three other children were captured.

Over the next two years, her family traveled, twice, to the distant canyons and mesas of Comancheria to try and rescue Matilda, but both attempts failed. During one try, Matilda's father spotted her in the Comanche camp but couldn't reach her amidst the chaos of the botched rescue attempt.

In 1840 a band of sixty Comanches rode into San Antonio to negotiate terms with the settlers. The Texans had requested that thirteen hostages be returned but the Comanches, hoping to negotiate better prices for the others, only brought one captive: Matilda Lockhart. They claimed that the others had run away.

The Texans were incensed when they saw Matilda's condition. She was covered in scars and her face was badly disfigured. They had burned off her nose and she spoke of the physical and sexual abuse she had suffered. Having learned some of the Comanche language while captive, she was able to tell the Texans that the Comanches were lying and hoping to increase their ransoms.

The Texans were livid and emotionally charged by Matilda's condition, and her testimony that other Texans were still being held against their will. Negotiations quickly faltered and fighting broke out inside the Council House in downtown San Antonio. In what would later be referred to as The Council House Fight, over thirty Comanches were killed, many of whom were established leaders in the tribe.

Captives that would later be rescued told the Texans that the surviving Comanches returned from the Council House Fight thoroughly wrought with anguish. The tribe wailed and grieved for days. An emerging Comanche warrior chief named Buffalo Hump vowed that he would one day seek revenge for The Council House Fight.

While Matilda was finally rescued by her family during the skirmish in San Antonio, she never recovered from the shame and lasting physical effects of her ordeal. She died at age eighteen, only three years after her return.

By 10 p.m. fatigue was again taking over and my mind began fabricating things that weren't there. Nighttime hallucinations were shockingly different than the ones in the stark light of day. Everything was magnified by the light from the bow. The trees were much taller in this section and a light breeze gave the visions more action and movement.

Phil must have succumbed at about the same time because he chimed in from the back of the boat, "Are you seeing things?"

"Yeah, it's creepy. I feel like we're in a Mardi Gras parade…or maybe it's the Chinese New Year?"

We were paddling through a corridor of monstrous characters and colorful creatures waving in slow motion and laughing. I saw jesters and knights in armor. There were fire breathing dragons and princesses with chiffon scarves flowing from their pointed hats.

Phil and I laughed while we compared apparitions. Oddly enough, it actually helped to keep the hallucinations under control when we talked about them. Most of the time we could see what the other was seeing but sometimes we laughed and tried to convince the other it was really something else.

"No, no, Christine, that's not a knight jousting on a horse, it's a two-headed tiger eating hay…can't you see it?"

We pulled into the Cuero 236 Checkpoint laughing and feeling pretty good. Sophie and my mom had gone to a motel for the night. Monica, Tom and my dad greeted us with cheers and then quieted down to business while we swapped out what little trash we'd created on that stretch.

I told Tom about the wonderful parade we had just paddled through and he looked at me like I was completely off my rocker. Which I guess I was.

It was dark so we didn't need the ice socks. We swapped out water jugs, and informed Monica that we planned to paddle straight to the Victoria Checkpoint, but not to worry if we were a little off pace. Rest stops were unavoidable at that point.

The team was upbeat. Everything went smoothly. We didn't even have to get out of the boat; it was a very efficient pit stop.

With that, we said goodbye to the ghosts of the Lockhart, Sutton, and Taylor families, and the others that we had fabricated along the route. We were bound for Victoria in the dead of night, ready for what we both thought was a more familiar section of the river.

## Cuero Checkpoint

| | |
|---|---|
| CUTOFF TIME: | MONDAY 10:00 P.M. |
| OUR TIME: | SUNDAY 10:30 P.M. |
| PLACE: | 47TH |
| TIME ELAPSED: | 37 HOURS AND 30 MINUTES |
| MILES PADDLED: | 160 |
| MILES TO GO: | 100 |

# CHAPTER 20

# CUERO TO VICTORIA

*"I love sleep. My life has the tendency to fall apart when I'm awake, you know?"*

–ERNEST HEMINGWAY

The forty miles between the Cuero and Victoria checkpoints is the same course that's used for the Safari Prelim Race each May. Banning and I did fairly well in that race, securing a starting position in the middle of the pack. Phil had raced with his former five-man team but they were so far ahead of us in the prelim we never saw him. He was on his way back to Austin by the time we arrived at the boat ramp in Victoria.

My recollection of this stretch was that it was fairly benign. I didn't recall any stressors, or portages. Phil agreed. We knew there were three of four sets of mild rapids as well as a few boils and sweepers. But we were excited to be back on the Prelim section.

We saw a few other teams here and there in the dark as we paddled. It was hard, though, to tell who was whom in the dark as people were keeping pretty quiet during the second night of the race. We passed a few teams that were pulling off to nap, and came alongside others that were done resting and pulling back into the race.

Midnight came after about six miles of paddling, and suddenly we were into Monday. At about that same time, Phil and I both noticed that we were getting loopy again. Not the bizarre hallucinations from the previous stretch, but weird sensations of blackness in front of us that made it feel like we were about to paddle off the edge of the Earth. It was terribly strange. We would be in a fairly placid, wide stretch of river and start to question where to go and what to do. It's a good thing Christopher Columbus had put that whole "earth is flat" idea to rest or we'd have been even more panicky.

We paddled on, but we were having trouble making out obstacles and exactly what was going on with the river. Our eyes weren't registering what was actually in front of us.

Does it look like the river goes to the right up ahead? Or... no, wait, that's a gravel bar. Are there dams in this section? No. But is that a dam? Are we about to go over it? It looks like a drop-off. At times we would literally back paddle and slow down.

No, it wasn't a dam. There were no dams in this section.

Phil voiced precisely what I was thinking, "This doesn't look anything like the Prelim race to me. I don't recognize anything."

"Me either. This seems completely different."

Of course, the Prelim was held during the day, after a decent night's sleep, and we hadn't already paddled 160 miles when that race started.

We were plugging along when we came upon a familiar blue and white boat and recognized Jamie and Brian. It was a welcomed treat to run into them, but they also seemed rather low on energy. We enjoyed some small talk for a little while but then they pulled ahead of us. Frankly it was nice to have them as a focal point, their boat was bright enough to see clearly and it was a relief each time they didn't paddle off what we thought looked like another dam that wasn't supposed to be there.

With a goal to keep them in sight, we picked up our stroke pace and began clipping along fairly fast. Phil and I were calling out obstacles to each other, communicating well. The current seemed to be picking up and we were only about twenty yards behind Jamie and Brian when they suddenly turned on a dime and cut hard left into a fast moving chute. We quickly followed them river left.

"Phil, ROCK!" was all I could manage.

I did an unauthorized draw stroke, and we missed it by mere inches. Paddling as aggressively as we could we entered the same chute behind Jamie and Brian with our boat tilted so far over that it felt like my elbow would graze the water. I really thought we were going to flip at the top of these rapids and wondered where they would eventually spit us out. Miraculously the boat did right itself, but we were still screaming along at a maddening clip. I'm still not sure if I was yelling aloud, or only in mind, but my heart was pounding wildly and I do vaguely remember Phil's shouts of "KEEP PADDLING!"

The fast moving rapids straightened out to a chute running alongside the left bank. I could see Jamie and Brian flying up ahead. Suddenly they disappeared to the right and I heard the sound of tree branches scraping against fiberglass.

"Phil, TREES!"

To this day, I still don't know how he did it, but Phil managed to steer us, unscathed and hauling ass, through a huge tangle of tall trees, downed trunks and overhanging branches. Astonishingly we punched through in one piece where we could see Jamie and Brian way downriver.

"Oh. My. Word!" I screamed over and over. "Great paddling Phil! Great steering! I can't believe you got us through there!"

"SHIT, that was wild!" he yelled, "I thought we were going over for sure. Good job paddling in the front!"

Thankfully we had reached another stretch of flat, calm water below the rapids so we could wind down and let the adrenaline flow back to wherever it goes. Again, we discussed that dreaded scenario of swimming hard to the bank to avoid strainers. Phil was still adamant about no life vests in those situations. After a few more minutes my heart rate began to slow back to normal when Phil said, "Oh and one more thing. If we go over in the dark, turn your headlamp on so I can find you if you're trapped underwater."

Good to know.

My heart was racing again and I nervously touched the headlamp which was actually around my neck. The elastic band was too tight on my forehead and since we only turned them on when we needed to check out something specific on the bank, I left it off and wore it around my neck so I wouldn't get a headache. Now I was nervous that it could get caught on an underwater tree branch, thus accelerating my demise. I was on full alert. In my mind I went over and over my action plan if we hit another rough spot.

We kept Jamie and Brian in our sights for about half an hour but eventually they pulled away from us. I was on point, focused and way too scared to hallucinate. I kept a keen eye for obstacles and tried to help Phil choose our lines, all while asking for a little help from above. I was too tired to conjure up anything intelligent or even coherent to say, so I stripped it down to the studs.

*Dear God, please give me what I need to paddle this section safely.*

I wasn't making deals. I didn't offer anything in return. I wasn't showing off insightful analysis or some great piece of wisdom I'd learned about life or parenting or the world or faith. I was just asking for a little help.

Phil would later say that this section scared him like no other in the race.

As we paddled on we tried to piece together what we knew, or thought we knew, about this forty-mile stretch. I remembered it was divided into thirds by two bridges. The Thomaston Bridge…had we already done that? We were getting so confused. And then there was that other bridge. And Nursery Rapids. Were there two sets of Nursery Rapids? Didn't we just do those? Were *those* Nursery Rapids? We both agreed that we were utterly confused and that it seemed the river had slipped in a whole extra set of rapids that didn't used to be there.

At about 3 a.m., we both had a fairly good hunch that we were through the worst of it. The river was wide and calm, again. It was pitch black but at least we could see clearly ahead of us with no weird dam-like edges to fall off of, and no more rushing chutes that might sweep us to our deaths.

My arms hurt. My shoulders were tired. The sleeves on Phil's shirt were too long and starting to annoy me. My tailbone had reached a new plateau of pain that I didn't think possible. But worse than all of that, I *really* wanted to go to sleep. The lack of obstacles in this stretch had lulled me back into that familiar dizzy, loopy dream state. If I stopped paddling for even a second I could look down at my hands and literally watch myself falling asleep.

*Wake up wake up wake up. Shake the head. Blink blink blink…*

Then I felt the boat jerk from the stern. Phil was falling asleep too. For some reason that made me perk up, like I had a new responsibility. It worked for a few minutes, but then I would nod off into a little mini paddling coma, jerking back to alertness just before I tumbled out of the boat. From my seat in the bow, I could also feel Phil's nods becoming more pronounced. A few times when he jerked back awake he rocked the boat so sharply I truly thought we were going over.

"Phil, I can't believe we are still upright. I can't believe we haven't fallen asleep and tumped the boat."

"Yeah, I'm tired."

"I think we should find a spot to nap."

"Cool."

My spirits buoyed. We were through the scariest part of this section. I wasn't drowning underwater, choking from my headlamp. I was alive, and looking for a napping spot.

But we couldn't find one.

My exhilaration soon waned as we paddled and paddled and paddled looking for a safe place to take the boat out. The banks were all too steep with heavy current moving along them. It was hard to see the opposite bank in the dark, so several times we actually paddled all the way across to flip on our headlights for a closer look.

Nope, too steep.

This went on and on, and we were wasting time and energy in our serpentine search for a napping spot.

"Are you kidding me?" I shouted into the night, "Phil, I am losing it! I can't believe we are doomed to bob on this water forever!"

"This is torture," Phil agreed.

Finally, at around 6 a.m. we found a nice gravel bar and a clean grassy opening at river left. Daylight was flooding back into the sky as we lugged the boat out of the water and onto the gravel bar. I found a lovely spot with small rocks and clean grass where I laid out my foam pad. I took off my shoes, covered my eyes with my hat and covered my nose and mouth with my nasty stinky Buff. I placed my life vest beneath my head and was out, immediately.

We probably slept for about 45 minutes. It was a great nap. I could have loitered in the REM stages much longer but a herd of chupacabras disguised as insects were taking blood donations from my face and hands and buzzing past my ears like fighter planes.

Phil spoke up, groggy and annoyed, "I'm getting eaten alive."

"They're awful. Should we get going?"

Even though we had slept for almost an hour, my muscles and joints screamed in protest when I stood to gather up my gear; they obviously wanted more rest. My back ached, my shoulders burned, and my rear-end was completely numb. But at that point we only had about six river miles left before the Victoria Checkpoint, and waking up after two nights on the river made me feel like we were actually making some progress. If we continued our current pace, there was a good chance that we'd be sleeping in a comfy motel at some point later that night.

As we put our shoes back on and re-packed the canoe, a male solo paddler pulled up to our spot. He looked completely worn down.

"Sorry," he apologized. "I didn't mean to crowd y'all out. I just thought it looked like a good bank."

"No worries," Phil assured him. "We were just on our way out."

I greeted him as I was putting my things into the boat. "It's a good spot to nap. Enjoy it. We spent about an hour trying to find a decent place to rest before we found this one."

The guy agreed but couldn't sustain the enthusiasm for a complete sentence. "Hey, you're not kidd…" His words trailed off as he trudged toward the napping spot.

Not long after we shoved off, we ran into a few other teams, including Sam Hilker. Phil was energized by the start of the day and the paddling company, "Hey guys, was that a wild night or what?"

We shared stories from the second night on the water. It was pretty much the same for everyone and we all had big laughs about certain places that almost tripped us up. Everyone had a turn at the podium to tell their version of coming upon that boulder at the top of the crazy rapids and tree-tunnel at river left. We were all laughing and cheering but deep down we all knew we were damn lucky to be safe with our boats in one piece.

We kept pace with Sam Hilker for a while and again Phil brought up the logjam and the cut into Alligator Lake. He recounted it back to her to make certain he had it right. I even articulated it a few times to make sure I understood.

The company was short-lived and by 7:30 a.m. we were paddling alone, again. As the sun climbed up over the tree tops the heat and humidity rose quickly to oppressive levels. Mildly refreshed from our nap, we were moving at a pretty decent clip when the hallucinations kicked in again. On the left side of the river, standing close to the bank I saw this extraordinary pink and white exotic bird. It was shaped sort of like a pelican, but too short for a flamingo.

I fully expected the cartoonish bird to vaporize as we got closer, but at fifty yards it was still there. Its bill was shaped like a soup ladle and its knees bent backward when it walked. It looked like an odd artistic marriage of John James Audubon and Dr. Seuss.

Finally I had to ask. "Uh, Phil. Do you see that pink bird?"

I waited for his response, which seemed to take a while.

"Yeah, what is that?"

"You see it too!"

We inched closer for a better look.

"That's not a pelican is it?"

"I have no idea," Phil shrugged.

At that point I began to look around and noticed the change in topography. Gone were the familiar rolling hills and towering pecan trees next to the river. We were in flat terrain and the riverbanks were lined with scraggly mesquites, retamas, and palms. There was prickly pear cactus and a distinctive familiar smell on the southeast breeze.

"I don't know what sort of weird hybrid bird it is, but I can tell you this, that bird is *coastal*. We are getting close to Seadrift!"

I would later learn that our glorious pink harbinger of coastal hope was a Roseate Spoonbill, and I can promise you that I will never look at another one without an overwhelming flood of sentiment.

At around 8:00 a.m. we rounded a bend and spotted the boat ramp at Victoria City Park. With about 60,000 residents Victoria is one of the larger towns on the Texas Coastal Bend. Situated at the confluence of three major highways, it's a two-hour drive from Austin, Houston, and San Antonio. As the crow flies, Victoria is only 30 miles from Seadrift, but we still had 60 river miles to paddle before the finish line.

It was from this point on the river that the Comanche Chief Buffalo Hump launched the Great Raid of 1840 in retaliation for The

Council House Fight. Following our same course down the Guadalupe, Buffalo Hump's band of 400 warriors raided and plundered through southeast Texas, vowing to drive the white man to the sea and stain the ocean red with his blood.

Victoria was the first city attacked. The Comanches managed to steal 1,500 horses, but they weren't able to kill as many settlers as they hoped. Apparently Buffalo Hump hadn't accounted for the fact that the Texans could simply lock their doors and shoot through cracked windows.

From Victoria the Comanches pushed south to the town of Linnville, close to modern day Port Lavaca. There, they unleashed hell. They burned and ransacked stores and houses, killed, tortured and captured a few settlers, and drove hundreds of Linnville residents onto their boats, fleeing for their lives into Lavaca Bay. Because Linnville was a port city, a local warehouse was storing an estimated $300,000 worth of goods at the time. The Comanches helped themselves to imported top hats, umbrellas, and calico dresses.

Their gluttony for fashion, captives, and Euro-bling ultimately stunted their raid when the Texans later caught up with the overloaded Comanches at Plum Creek and gave them a payback for the Victoria and Linnville attacks.

While researching details of the Great Raid, I learned that, today, Buffalo Hump actually has his own Facebook page. Given that his Comanche name *Po-cha-na-quar-hip* means "erection that won't go down," you'd think he would have more than just two fans.

With the Victoria Checkpoint in view, Phil began to outline our plan. "We're doing pretty well on time. Let's take a few minutes to get things organized. Let's get trash out of the boat. Square things up just the way we want them. Use the port-a-potty. Apply Desitin. This is our last major pit stop."

We pulled into the boat ramp and Monica met us with smiles and her consistent calm, organized demeanor. My dad and Tom were there along with Shea McClanahan, a Hill Country fly-fishing guide who was team captain for friends Max and Mike. Apparently they had pulled out of Victoria just minutes before we arrived. Shea was on his own without support and it was clear he was enjoying the fellowship of the Team Paddlefish crew.

Though physically worn down, we were emotionally charged as we readied ourselves for the final legs of the race. I gave Phil his shirt back and found my spare blue shirt in its vacuum package; fresh, clean and with sleeves the right length. Perfection. I mixed Cytomax into my new water jug, checked my food supply, and cleared out the trash in the bow. When Phil returned from the port-a-potty he handed me the tube of Desitin like it was a race baton. I scurried up the hill for my designated leg of the monkey butt relay.

We were fired up leaving Victoria. Spirits were high and Seadrift was coming into focus. About five minutes after we left the Victoria Checkpoint, we saw several more Roseate Spoonbills standing in a marshy area, river right.

"I love those crazy pink birds!"

## Victoria Checkpoint

| | |
|---|---|
| CUTOFF TIME: | TUESDAY 11:00 A.M. |
| OUR TIME: | MONDAY 8:31 A.M. |
| PLACE: | 44TH |
| TIME ELAPSED: | 47 HOURS AND 31 MINUTES |
| MILES PADDLED: | 200 |
| MILES TO GO: | 60 |

# CHAPTER 21

# Victoria to Dupont

*"I feel monotony and death to be almost the same."*
–Charlotte Bronte

My euphoria dissipated completely not long after we left Victoria. The river flow slowed down and there wasn't the faintest hint of a breeze. It seemed we were paddling in slow motion.

My body wasn't recovering as well as it had earlier in the race. An hour of rest wasn't enough for my shoulders, fanny, or knees. I was tired. My blood felt thin and useless. My brain was cloaked in a steaming fog. The scant tree line and cloudless sky allowed every last ray of sunlight to beat down upon us. How could it be this muggy so early in the morning? I felt about as nimble and zippy as a mastodon stuck in a bubbling tar pit.

With no other racers in sight, the trek to Dupont began to feel a lot like yesterday's death march to Hochheim. We were lonely, hot, and bored. The mere thought of our once-favorite team songs made me want to throw up. There was literally no conversation topic that we hadn't already covered. It would have to be incredibly juicy and interesting at this point if I was going to waste the physical energy and calories to speak.

We had to dip in the water regularly to cool down and wake up. Mildly refreshed after one of these swim breaks I figured this was my best opportunity to try and chat.

"So Phil. Where do you think some of the other teams are right about now?"

"Well, we know the Belizean team is finished."

"Yeah. What about like West and Katie, Bugge and Meagan, and The Hippie Chicks?"

"The Hippie Chicks should finish around 60-65 hours. Maybe less? I don't know. They trained hard."

"What about your friend who broke his rudder."

"Charlie?"

"Yeah, him."

"Dunno."

"So what about Erin Magee? We haven't heard any mention of her?"

"No clue, but she should be finishing soon."

Erin is another legendary paddler within the Safari hierarchy. In her early Safari years she raced on large teams, but recently she's been paddling solo, and doing quite well. At some of the prelim races she took considerable time with Banning and me, talking us through different parts of the race route and the importance of paddling form. She oozes a never say die attitude and during one training run she told us, "I have a deal with my team captains. Don't ever tap me out at a checkpoint. I may seem loopy and totally out of it, but I don't care how sick and tired I look, don't tap me out, no matter what. I'm known for just paddling on."

Erin has her own thread on the Safari message board where she organizes training runs, open to anyone and everyone. She would pick a section of the river, name the time, and help organize shuttles. Banning and I participated in her bay training run in May. It was invaluable to have actually experienced the Guadalupe Delta, the bay crossing, and the actual finish line on the seawall in Seadrift.

"Hut."

By 9:30 a.m. our conversation had fizzled and I was back to focusing on my own personal torment. My left knee hurt from pressing against the foot plate in the bow. It was impossible to maintain good paddling form without using my legs and feet for leverage. I tried shifting my weight and occasionally lifting my left foot from the plate, but that only gave me a few seconds of relief.

"This is horrible!" I screamed out to no one in particular.

No acknowledgement from the stern.

The first exciting thing that happened (and I use that term generously) was paddling beneath the Hwy 175 bridge. We reached it around 10:30 a.m. and I chimed in with another of my textbook Safari insights, "Oh hey...I remember them talking about this at the Safari Seminar. From the 175 bridge there are 175 turns until Dupont. They said we should count them to stay entertained."

As predicted, the river was winding and turning in crazy hairpin loops. Apparently this section has been known to drive people completely mad. They think the checkpoint is just up ahead, but the turns slow things down for hours and hours on end.

I understand the topographical reasons that rivers serpentine through a delta as they near the shore, but I still find it strange that the river starts curving so aggressively at this late point. You'd think after all of this, after coming such a long way to reach the coast, it would be heading for the Gulf in a straightaway dead run like a horse heading for the stable. Was the Guadalupe stalling? Showing off? Perhaps this was the river's swan song before joining the sea and ceasing to exist.

Trying to account for all 175 turns, I counted the curves in my mind for a while. But then I lost count and abandoned the game altogether. It was like the Safari version of *Ninety-nine Bottles Of Beer On The Wall*, a fun idea that quickly turned insufferable.

I was dying. I couldn't tell if I was dying of exhaustion, pain, or boredom, but I was pretty sure I was dying. My paddling form had collapsed along with my mental fortitude. We needed company—paddlers, an animal, anything to break up the monotony.

"Where are those damn famous alligators?" I pondered aloud. "Everyone swore there would be tons of them south of Victoria."

"We'll see them at night, closer to the bay."

A set of rapids would have been good at this point. Or maybe a big, loud and scary Comanche raid, especially if they were well-dressed like those that plundered Linnville. I'd hate to be scalped by a Comanche that didn't take pride in his warring attire.

I reached up and felt my long braid. Maybe they'd note my black hair and dark complexion and spare me as one of their own? I didn't want to think about what was living inside the braid in my hair. Ticks, cobwebs, twigs, bits of dried cow dung. Meanwhile I really hoped I didn't have a zit. It was weird not to know what was going on with my face. No mirror for three days. The reality sunk in.

*Oh no, please don't let me have a huge, honking zit…*

When we were at the Victoria Checkpoint I applied two dollops of sunscreen to the tops of my hands but forgot to re-apply on my nose.

*I hope it's not sunburned…*

I pulled my Buff from my neck up and over my nose to keep the sun off, but the rank odor was too much. I wished I had brought a spare.

At 10:45 a.m., Phil interrupted my mental rambling.

"Do you hear that?"

"Indians? Alligators? What?" My imagination had taken my sanity hostage.

"No, people…voices."

Then I heard them, two men talking. We needed company; we paddled faster.

Around the next bend we came up behind my friends Max and Mike from Austin. It was odd that we were just then seeing them for the fist time. We would later learn how close we had been with them throughout the race.

It was great to finally have company but, unfortunately, I was hitting a wall. Or, as Phil called it, I was "bonking big time." I was in a daze. I wasn't at all chatty. My shoulders were mush and my paddle strokes were pitiful. My elbows seemed practically pinned next to my ribcage as I went through a truncated version of the textbook paddling motion. I looked like the cheapskate check-dodger at a group dinner. I've often heard that person described as having "alligator arms," short and dysfunctional appendages that make it difficult to reach for a restaurant tab or a wallet.

"Hey…have y'all seen any alligators?"

Mike shook his head and Max answered, "No, not yet."

We talked about the crazy night between Cuero and Victoria. We traded stories about how and when we'd hit different sets of rapids. We worked our way backwards up the race route, comparing notes on Gonzales, Ottine, and Staples Dam. We reminisced about the crowds and the spectators and the noise from day one. We all agreed it seemed like a lifetime ago.

From there our conversation turned to the various cuts and creeks that supposedly flowed to and from the river on this leg from Victoria to Dupont.

Max asked, "Have we already gone by Cornfield Cut?"

"I'm not sure," said Phil.

I added, "I don't think so. I haven't seen anything coming in or out."

At around 11 a.m. we veered left avoiding a passage that we assumed was Cornfield Cut. At 11:30 a.m. we passed another one called Blue Bayou cut. Fortunately the main river was still plainly defined and there was no confusion at either place. Unfortunately, however, the mere mention of Blue Bayou set my mind to methodically spinning Linda Ronstadt lyrics that I couldn't seem to shake.

Phil asked Max and Mike, "So how are y'all liking your first Safari?"

Max, "Oh man, we love it. This is the coolest adventure. We're already ready for next year, talking about what we're going to tweak."

"Will you go aluminum again?"

"Oh yeah, this is our boat. We bought it. We'll paddle in this again for sure."

We ventured on talking about the Safari, boat materials, paddle length, training strategies. Phil led the dialogue with Max and Mike; he was at his best in these conversations about paddling, racing, and gear. I was delighted to listen and have a distraction that didn't require much of me. I just paddled and nodded and smiled every now and again. Physically, this was my lowest point in the race, and I was glad to have the surrounding conversation to keep me from dwelling on how bad I was hurting.

Just as he had with nearly everyone we had encountered along the way, Phil then brought up the one obstacle that we were both still worried about. "Have y'all heard anything about the big logjam down in the next section?"

Mike said, "Just that it's still there. About a mile long. What about y'all?"

We concurred. Phil told stories of the hell he went through last year doing the one mile portage around the logjam and how his team accidentally missed a point to re-enter the river, adding a couple of hundred yards to the grueling hike.

We shared the intel we'd received from Sam Hilker about the cut into Alligator Lake. They seemed very interested so Phil explained in detail. "When you see the first logjam, cut right immediately. Hug the land on your left and don't ever go into the main part of Alligator Lake. When it ends you spit back into the main river on the left below the biggest logjam."

Like us, they asked questions and wanted to go over it a few times. Even I stepped them through it having heard it so many times myself. Plus I wanted to practice in my own mind and make sure I had it memorized in case Phil was out of it or needed to confer with me once we were down there.

Every so often Phil would gently nudge me into higher gear by paddling harder from the stern. It was a subtle way of lighting a fire under a droopy bowman and I responded well to this method. We'd pull ahead from Max and Mike for a bit just to get the blood flowing and then Phil would say quietly, "If it's alright with you I'm gonna drop back and paddle with them again. I think we need to conserve energy and I think we need the company."

"Oh yeah, that's fine. I agree."

This was our cyclical pattern for miles and miles. Around 12:30 p.m. Max pointed at a tributary that was flowing into the Guadalupe at river right and said, "Hey, I guess that's Coleto Creek."

In 1836, this narrow tributary was the scene of another pivotal battle in Texas' revolution against Mexico. It ended in tragedy for the Texans, but sparked an intense furor that ultimately led to Texas sovereignty.

On March 19th, just two weeks after the fall of the Alamo, Colonel James Fannin and his troops met an army of 900 Mexican soldiers on the banks of Coleto Creek, just a few miles upstream from where it merges with the Guadalupe.

Mexican General Jose Urrea ordered his troops to advance on the Texans, but Fannin's men fought valiantly even though they were greatly outnumbered. Urrea lost over a hundred men and was running out of ammunition, but Fannin's troops were low on water and a cold drizzle made it difficult to light fires at night to treat their wounded. At dawn Fannin surrendered to Urrea in exchange for leniency. Urrea promised that if Fannin and his troops would return as prisoners to Fort Defiance in Goliad, they would ultimately be released.

Unfortunately, Urrea's boss, the narcissistic Santa Anna disagreed with this plan and cruelly ordered Urrea to kill the 342 Texas soldiers. Urrea wanted no part of this execution and campaigned on behalf of Fannin and his men. His pleas were denied, and on March 27th 1836, Palm Sunday, Fannin and his men were led out of Fort Defiance in three columns, each column surrounded by two rows of Mexican soldiers. They were shot point blank. Survivors were clubbed and knifed. Twenty-eight feigned death and escaped. Fannin was killed last, after watching his men die. He was seated in a chair, blindfolded, and shot in the face.

News of the Goliad Massacre spread quickly, and three weeks later a small band of defiant Texans led by Sam Houston surprised Santa Anna's massive force while they were napping on the banks of the San Jacinto River, near present day Deer Park. Under a collective battle cry of "Remember Goliad! Remember the Alamo!" Houston's men killed over 600 Mexican soldiers in only eighteen minutes, and forced the surrender of Santa Anna. Three weeks later he begrudgingly signed the peace treaty that ultimately led to Texas' designation as an independent republic.

Not long after passing Coleto Creek, we reached a logjam in the dead center of the river, with a seam of current flowing on either side. It didn't appear to require a portage but we were confused as to which way to go. The river appeared to fork on the other side of the massive tangle, and if we chose the wrong route, we could end up in a dead-end cut or paddling into some endless maze of stagnant creeks. But both paths looked pretty equal; it was like a giant watery wishbone and we desperately needed to pull the bigger leg.

The four of us paddled slowly, even trying to paddle backwards in order to give ourselves more time to choose. It was a tough call. The consensus vote was finally the left side and luckily we chose well. The river kept moving and so did we.

Around 1:30 p.m. we started to question how much further to the Dupont Checkpoint. Phil compared our GPS to the reading on Max and Mike's GPS. There were discrepancies, which was confounding.

Phil asked, "Did we pass it?"

It seems like a ridiculous question in the middle of nowhere with no other structure, bridges or activity to compete for our attention. You'd think a checkpoint would stand out. But when you've been paddling for days without proper sleep and broiling your brain in the hot Texas sun, questions like these start to make sense.

"Surely we didn't pass it," I said.

We paddled for a while in silence.

"Where the hell is it? Which side of the river is it on?" asked Phil.

"I think it's on the left."

Finally we rounded turn number 175 at 2:30 p.m. and saw Tom at river left. He and Shea were kicked back in folding chairs in the shade and drinking a beer. They leapt into action, cheering wildly, folding up their chairs and running alongside us. They shouted downriver to the rest of the team, "They're here! They're coming in!"

The Dupont Checkpoint is scrappy at best. We dunked our bodies into the muddy water to cool off and floated weightlessly for a few minutes to relieve our aching joints. Sophie came down from where the cars were parked and yelled, "Hey Mommy! Look what I caught!" She was wearing a Texas Water Safari t-shirt and holding up a giant rubber snake, both of which her grandmother had no doubt purchased somewhere along the race route.

I loved their team spirit.

My dad and Tom were in business mode, helping Monica take trash, trade ice socks and swap water jugs. My dad and Tom were unshaven and their scraggly beards reminded me how long we'd been out here. I could only imagine what I looked like.

After the water transfers, Phil addressed the team. "We're in the final stretches now. Two more legs. With this pace we are tracking for a 62-68 hour finish. Which means we'll reach Seadrift in the middle of the night."

Monica knew right where he was heading with this. "Tell me what y'all want to eat and we'll go ahead and have it waiting for you. There are microwaves at the motel so probably best if you order something that reheats well."

Phil ordered Asian food and I ordered Italian. Seadrift pretty much only had two restaurant options and both were seafood—fried, of course—which didn't appeal to us at the time. Monica and the team assured us they would scour surrounding towns for Asian and Italian takeout. I think my mom was fired up to be a part of this important task.

Meanwhile I couldn't believe the conversation we were having. Italian food. A bed. A/C. The next time we laid down it would be in an artificially-refrigerated motel room with piles of cheesy carbohydrates and the cable TV blaring.

*God Bless America!*

It may have still been twelve hours from my grasp but it was a big carrot. A HUGE carrot!

Max and Mike were still floating and resting at 2:51 p.m. when Phil announced we were pulling out of Dupont. As we paddled away into the searing mid-day heat of July 12, 2010, I wondered if they would get me spaghetti or fettuccine. Marinara or cream sauce? Ooh, maybe chicken parmesan? It didn't matter. I planned to eat Italian food every day for a week after this race, so whatever they didn't get me I would easily cover in the seven-day gluttony fest that would follow the Safari.

But secretly I was hoping for chicken parmesan.

## Dupont Checkpoint

| | |
|---|---|
| CUTOFF TIME: | TUESDAY 10:00 P.M. |
| OUR TIME: | MONDAY 2:51 P.M. |
| PLACE: | 41ST |
| TIME ELAPSED: | 53 HOURS AND 51 MINUTES |
| MILES PADDLED: | 228 |
| MILES TO GO: | 32 |

# CHAPTER 22

# Dupont to Saltwater Barrier

*"If you are going through Hell, keep going."*
—Winston Churchill

After so many miles of paddling desolate uninhabited waters, it was nice to again see the occasional river house on the stretch between Dupont and the Saltwater Barrier. Most of those homes were built on tall pilings, another positive indication that we were well into the coastal flood plain.

At around 3:30 p.m. we paddled by a group of people cooking out and drinking beer on their back porch. They cheered and we smiled back. Phil had a brief visit with one of the guys and saw it as another chance to gather intel, "Hey, what's the deal with the logjam down here?"

"Aw, it's gone. Y'all are in great shape!"

We paddled onward, not sure we believed him but hoping he was right.

Soon after, I saw a house on the left that was set back from the river. It looked nice. Clean paint. A big iron Texas star affixed to the back porch.

*What is this nice house doing here? It's so big. Is it a home or a business?*

As we paddled closer I had a better chance to check it out.

"Oh my gosh…I've been there!"

Phil didn't react.

"Really. I've been there! I don't know how to tell you how random this is but I swear I've been to this place."

I can understand why Phil wasn't impressed. Most Safari racers had pounded both the water and the pavement all along these rivers, frequenting every Buc-ee's package store, every taco truck, and every restaurant from San Marcos to Seadrift. Getting the restaurant intel for these small towns along the race route was almost as important as getting mileage charts, gear lists, logjam updates and portage strategies.

On that note, I don't recommend ordering grilled chicken at the Gonzales Livestock Auction & Market. Bad move on my part to order poultry in a café that's physically attached to a stockyard.

About five years before, I was traveling around the state for a series of executive conferences for Leadership Texas and the Foundation for Women's Resources. As part of the agenda, I would lead multi-day seminars on strategic branding, messaging, and ways to grow their business.

For this particular gig I was due to present at one of their conferences in Corpus Christi. I was driving down and found myself starving in a relatively sparse area south of Victoria. Exiting the highway, I found a little grocery store with a few provisions on the shelves, all of which were labeled in Spanish. There was a tiny burger counter at the back with a couple of booths.

After my delicious greasy burger lunch I tried to get back on the highway, but the onramp was under construction. I drove along the frontage road for what seemed like eternity, seeing no one and grateful it was the middle of the afternoon, not dark. It was getting lonely out there and I was a tad concerned about finding the interstate again.

Right after I passed a large vulture eating the carcass of a feral hog in the center of the road, this nice little homey establishment popped up on the frontage road. The very one we'd just paddled by. It was like a swanky country grocery store turned icehouse. There were motorcycles parked out front and people eating and drinking on the porch and picnic tables. Vintage country music was playing. The vibe was super friendly and oh so Texas. I loved it. I hung out for a while and lamented the fact that I needed to find the highway and get to Corpus.

I laughed and thought about that business trip as we paddled past that cool old joint. How far away was *that* life right now? I remember spending my days in a hotel conference room with a headset mic talking to hundreds of hot shot female execs who are probably running their own companies by now.

I paddled on, thinking of how odd this change of perspective was. When I stopped into that place five years ago, I don't even recall noticing that there was a river out back.

I considered eating up some time explaining the story to Phil but decided it was too hard to convey the serendipity of it all, and I really didn't have the energy to do it justice.

"Hut!"

I switched sides and changed topics.

"So do you think that guy was right? Do you think the logjam is gone?"

"I doubt it. I hope so, but I doubt it."

As usual Phil was right. At about nine miles into this section, around 5 p.m., we paddled around a gentle curve and there it was.

"Whoa!" Phil said. "Let's slow down and see what we've got."

We drifted along slowly and bought ourselves some thinking time as we studied the massive obstacle.

He asked, "Think that's it?"

"Looks like a logjam to me, and I don't see a way through."

There were trunks and logs and branches piled fifteen to twenty feet high. It stretched across the entire river. As we drifted closer we could see an opening where part of the river peeled off to the right.

"There it is," I pointed. "There's the cut Sam told us to take."

"You think so?"

"I think it has to be. It's a giant logjam. And a cut to the right, just like she described."

"I think so, too. You ready for this? Should we take her plan?"

"Yeah, that's what we've been planning on, so let's do it."

Phil guided us into the creek that angled off to the right. What we hadn't anticipated was a minefield of debris: stickups, limbs, and logjam leftovers that had floated into the cut. We slowed down to avoid puncturing the boat.

"How are we going to zigzag through here—and how did Wade Binion get through here?" I asked.

"Don't' know..." Phil's voice trailed off as he focused on how to get through it. We tried to paddle but the water was so littered with debris that our paddles were basically knocking into stumps and limbs with each stroke. More than paddling we were poling through.

"Damn!" Phil was getting frustrated. "This is a nightmare."

We hacked away for a bit longer, but then we decided to punt.

Phil said it first, "I feel like we're gonna get stuck in here."

"I know. I'm not feeling good about this." We were pretty much sitting still at that point.

Phil called it, "Abort. This isn't working." I'm not going through all this junk just to get into Alligator Lake and potentially get lost. Are you okay doing the big portage and staying with the main river?"

"Yeah, let's get out of here." We turned around and picked our way back through the maze of logs and sticks. We were both worried about the boat. It felt like we were a cotton ball being pulled through a tangle of barbed wire.

When we got back to the mouth of the cut, Phil got out of the boat to size up our options. After a few minutes he re-emerged from the brush with a plan. "Here's the problem. We're on the right bank, but there's no good place to portage on this side. We need to portage on the left bank, but there's too much current for us to paddle straight across from here without getting sucked into the logjam."

"Okay."

"We'll need to carry the boat about a hundred yards back up-river on this side to give ourselves the best shot to cross with plenty of room above the logjam."

"Okay."

Phil was zoned in and firing on all cylinders and I was 100% on board with whatever he came up with to get us out of this. There was an air of gravitas and urgency. I knew at the very least that this portage was going to be tough, and possibly a complete debacle. There were so many hard luck stories about these logjam portages. One wrong move could cost us hours to correct. We already had to rewind from one bad decision and I wanted to be done with this before sunset.

We got the boat out of the water without much problem, but were quickly reminded of the old rancher adage that so aptly describes the South Texas Brush Country: an unforgiving land where everything either sticks, bites, scratches, or stings.

Within seconds of hauling the boat out I stepped in a fire ant mound, and as is normally the case, they didn't call out the signal to "BITE!" until they had completely swarmed my ankle. I trudged on with our portage and gritted my teeth while trying to use my other foot to scrape them off.

The banks were a tangled mess of mesquite, prickly pear, catclaw, and some type of low, clumpy vine with needle-like thorns. They looked like blackberry vines, but I didn't see any fruit. It was slow-going, and we literally had to hack and claw our way along the bank.

Adding to this unpleasant mix of fauna were clouds of mosquitoes the size of hummingbirds. They were rising from the brush and attacking us in swarms.

As we neared the point where Phil wanted to put the boat in, we heard voices on the river that we recognized.

"Damn," Phil said. "That's Max and Mike and we told them about the cut on the right. We need to let them know not to take it."

We left the boat where it was and hustled up the right bank so we could wave them down and give them enough reaction time. Sure enough they were hugging the right side, near us, and preparing to take the cut into Alligator Lake.

We started yelling, "Don't take the cut! Portage left!"

Thankfully they saw us quickly enough and had enough time to paddle across the river to the left bank. We watched them as they stopped to pull their boat out. There was a lot of yelling, and I'm not exactly sure who was saying what, but there was urgency and the tone was tough. "Come on man, get up on the bank! Come on! Get up there!"

I knew what great friends and race partners Max and Mike were, and suddenly I felt bad. I guess this is just the way guys talk to each other in these situations? Perhaps I had judged Phil too harshly for barking at me during this race.

I wasn't challenging him now, though. He was our problem-solver extraordinaire and I was beyond thrilled to have him as my teammate.

Phil said, "It's deep and fast where they are. See how hard they're working to get the boat out of the water? After we get the boat back in, we'll have to paddle upriver so we don't float down too close to the logjam while we're trying to pull the boat out."

The downside to this meant a longer portage down the left bank, but the water was just too fast near the logjam and we didn't want to get sucked into the pile. After sliding the boat back into the water, we stepped in and paddled upstream until we were well above the logjam. After shooting across to the left bank, I made an attempt to jump out and secure the bow on the bank, but the current was still too fast. We had to do a one-eighty, paddle back upriver and try again. Thankfully we finally found a spot along the left bank where the current was a bit more forgiving. I held onto some brush while Phil got out of the boat. He took the bow rope and tied it to a mesquite further up the slope.

"Okay, now you get out."

I got out and we hung on to the bowline as the stern began to swing around downriver. We had no room to stand in the thick, thorny brush, and no clear path to haul the boat out, but we had to do it quickly before the stern swung completely downriver.

When the current swung the boat to the point that it was perpendicular to the bank, we dug in with our heels and began pulling with everything we had. It took a lot of heaving, grunting, and cussing, but we finally got it wedged on the bank between two clumps of brush and out of the current. We stood for a moment, sweating profusely and trying to catch our breath, and then Phil suggested, "Let's walk down and see what we should do next."

After only a few yards of pushing through the dense thorn brush, I was wishing I had asked for a machete for Mother's Day. I couldn't think of anything I needed more at that time. We were on the crest of a small hill running parallel to the river and trying to hack our way through a dense maze of thorns, vines, cobwebs, and wasp nests.

Once we forced our way through the thicket, we found a marshy clearing below the hill with ankle deep water. It was warm and nasty, but ideal for dragging a boat. Even a little bit of water could help lighten the load.

We paused for a bit to rest and scout the best path for pulling the boat through the marsh. I was starting to think like Phil because I anticipated his next command. "Let's go back and get the boat down here."

After returning through the thicket back to the boat, we were able to find subtle gaps where we could work it through the tangle. Not actual lanes, mind you, just places where the brush was less dense than others. It was slow going.

About halfway through the thicket we reached a gap in the brush and saw Jamie and Brian, the father/son team, hauling their boat out of the river. They were struggling with the nasty brush as well.

As we pushed on through the thicket, Phil barked at me, "Don't push! Don't push! Hold on." He repositioned and tweaked our angle as I tried to lift and push the boat at just the right speed and pressure.

At the edge of the clearing we set the boat down and took a breather. I looked at Phil and then down at myself. We were covered in cobwebs, burrs and scratches.

Phil said, "Okay, I'm gonna let you walk down and see if you can find a good spot below the logjam where we can get the boat back in the river. Obviously a spot where the bushes give us an opening is best."

"No problem, I'm on it."

I footslogged through the marsh and was glad to be out of the thicket. With a small ridge and heavy brush to my right, I couldn't even see the river. This was going to take awhile.

I kept going and going. I was pretty sure I had made it below the logjam, but I couldn't find a clear spot that we could drag the boat through. Max and Mike were several hundred yards ahead and carrying their canoe way far left into a wooded area with tall liveoaks. They yelled back at me, "This way! This way back into the river!"

It looked much farther than I wanted to drag our boat, so I pushed on hoping to find something closer. Suddenly Brian appeared out of nowhere, running toward me.

"Hey we found a spot to get the boat back in. It's actually not that far down." He pointed downriver to a place that looked a lot closer than Max and Mike way off in the distance. He walked back upriver with me as I returned to Phil, and then it occurred to me that he was going the wrong way.

"Brian, why are you headed this way if y'all found a place to get the boat in down below?"

Sheepishly he answered, "Oh, I forgot my paddle up here when we were taking the boat out."

I smiled and we trudged back through the marsh toward Phil and our boat. I explained the plan to Phil while Brian peeled off and looked for his paddle in the brush.

Phil and I grabbed each side of the bow and dragged the canoe through the marsh. It wasn't easy, by any stretch, but the ankle-deep water did help lighten the load. All told we probably dragged it about half a mile before we spotted a clearing on the bank and saw Jamie sitting in his canoe, waiting for Brian to return.

We eased our boat down to the water and took a minute to relax and chat with Jamie. I thanked him profusely for sharing this spot with us.

"No problem," Jamie replied. "Happy to help."

When Brian returned with his paddle, both boats shoved off and turned downriver.

Physically I felt awful. My muscles were limp and I was itching all over. Emotionally, though, I was in good spirits. Phil and I were really in a groove and Team Paddlefish was on its way to the finish line.

"So do you think that's it? Is that the worst of the logjams?" Obviously I knew he didn't have a definitive answer but I was curious what he was thinking.

"I don't know. If Sam's information is right, there are two more smaller ones."

Max and Mike had re-entered the river and all three boats were now traveling in loose formation.

After another half-mile we reached the second logjam and it turned out that Sam was spot-on. We hooked and crooked our way through a labyrinth of logs and crud, but we never had to get out of the boat. A little limbo action, a little pushing off with the hands, but we broke free fairly easily and paddled on.

A bit further down we reached the third logjam, which was even smaller than the first two. We saw an opening river right with one smooth log laying just a few inches above the surface.

"Paddle hard." Phil said. "Paddle hard and we can jump it."

We dug in and increased our speed. The bow made it up and over but then we got stuck. Fortunately, the boat stopped with me sitting right above the log, so I hopped out and stood on it to lighten the load. While Phil paddled from the stern, I worked the boat over the log with my hands.

A flood of relief finally washed over us both when I climbed back in (without tumping) and we paddled away from the third log-jam. Over the span of a year, the mystery and threat of this particular obstacle had grown to near mythical proportion. I was excited to have it behind me.

After another hour, or so, the three boats spread out again and we found ourselves alone in the broiling heat. I couldn't keep track of which shoulder was giving me the most trouble. It kept shifting. For a while it was the left one, then it was the right.

I sipped on my drinking tube and snacked to keep my energy up. The portage had burned a lot of calories.

"Are you hallucinating at all?"

Phil said, "No. Not today."

"Me either. Don't you think that's kind of strange? How we both zoned out at the same time? And it's funny how when there's something important going on, like rapids or logjams, the hallucinations disappear."

"They'll be back."

And he was right. As the saying goes: an idle mind is the Devil's workshop.

It was dusk when we paddled up to the Saltwater Barrier. It's a strange structure that spans the river and looks like a bridge. It's used to keep saltwater from intruding too far upriver, which ensures adequate fresh water for irrigation and municipal water for the city of Victoria. During hurricane surges, it can be raised and lowered according to the tide level.

We were pumped up and in great spirits as we approached the checkpoint located just above the barrier. The soft evening light gave the whole scene an added sense of drama. This was it: our last official stop before the finish.

"Can you believe it?" Phil asked. "We're doing good. We shouldn't take too long, though, since we'll be crossing the bay at night."

"Got it. But I am hurting pretty badly. Can I just have five-ten minutes to lie down and stretch?"

"Yeah, that's cool. I need you at top-notch. We've still got several miles of river before we hit the bay. I don't remember this section very well, so I'm gonna need you."

"Okay. I just need a few minutes."

"No worries. You lie down, stretch, whatever. I'll get the light on the boat. Plus let's give Monica anything we no longer need. Anything we can do to lighten the load will help us in the bay."

"Cool."

As we pulled up, there was a quiet celebratory tone with an eerie overlay. I was pretty whipped and didn't feel too sure-footed as I got out of the boat. Monica was there with the water jugs, and Tim Cole was snapping photos and collecting video footage. I looked back at Phil to make sure I wasn't skipping out on my share of any work. He nodded at me to go on. He was in a great mood.

I wanted to make full use of my time so I quickly told my dad and Tom that I was going to lie down for a second. First, I made a stop at the port-a-potty, then I found a patch of soft grass where I could stretch out. I closed my eyes and could hear light murmurings from the crowd at the water's edge. There were a lot of officials at this checkpoint. I suppose it was pretty exciting to see the teams come through this spot. Lying down felt good, but the excitement was overriding my need to rest. I stood up and walked around in circles to get the blood flowing. I stretched my arms, rolled my neck around and pulled on my shoulders to try and offer them some relief.

I walked back over to the boat and our team. Phil was chipper and fired up. I helped unload unnecessary items from the boat and put it all on the ground for Monica. I gave her my hat, sunglasses, extra Cytomax packets, extra food. Phil advised that we calculate the exact number of snacks we would need to make it to the finish line, then add some in case we got stuck in the bay. We had spare sunglasses and hats squirreled away in Seal-a-meal pouches as a last resort.

As we were purging the final bits and pieces we could live without, Max and Mike paddled into the checkpoint. We waved and cheered. Max smiled but Mike trudged off toward the port-a-potty. Max said, flatly, "He's not feeling so great."

We nodded.

As we prepared to shove off I looked around and then took in a big breath of humid, salty air. It felt great to be so close to the finish. We said our final farewells to our team.

"This is it." Phil said.

"Next stop Seadrift." my dad added.

The restrained excitement that we all shared was indescribable. Even the claps and cheers seemed to have a unique and distinct sound as we pulled away.

As we paddled beneath the barrier, I noticed that the wind

was blowing for the first time in this race. Where was this breeze during those long and punishing afternoons without shade? It felt good on my face and reminded me of redfish trips on the coast.

Naively I enjoyed the wind thinking it was nothing more than a perfunctory "Welcome to the Coast" billboard.

*Oh, it always blows like this down here...nothing to worry about...we're nearly done!*

## Saltwater Barrier Checkpoint

| | |
|---|---|
| CUTOFF TIME: | WEDNESDAY 8:00 A.M. |
| OUR TIME: | MONDAY 8:22 P.M. |
| PLACE: | 41ST |
| TIME ELAPSED: | 59 HOURS AND 22 MINUTES |
| MILES PADDLED: | 244 |
| MILES TO GO: | 16 |

# CHAPTER 23

# SALTWATER BARRIER TO GUADALUPE BAY

*"A great wind is blowing, and that gives you either imagination or a headache."*
–CATHERINE THE GREAT

We still had some light in the sky when we left the Saltwater Barrier. As massive as the Guadalupe River had been in places, it was ironic to me that in its final moments, it funneled down to one of the most narrow passages we'd paddled during the entire race.

We faced ten more miles in the river before reaching the mouth. After that, it was an estimated six miles of open bay until Seadrift. The actual finish line was a set of steps on the seawall near the flagpole and city park pavilion.

I was excited, but nervous. I couldn't believe we were going to be crossing the bay at night. I'd heard so many tales of racers becoming disoriented in the daytime. Teams that had overshot Seadrift and paddled back up the seawall to approach the finish line from the south. Teams that had been blown back up to the mouth of the bay over and over again. Exhausted racers tumping over in big waves and clinging to their boats awaiting rescue.

In 1998 a solo paddler named Richard Steppe flipped in the

bay. He removed his life vest and put it in the boat so he could swim faster, but somehow lost his grip and the wind carried his boat away. He was in the bay for nine hours without food or water but managed to swim all the way to Seadrift, walk up the seawall steps and cross the official finish line.

Unfortunately he didn't receive a patch because Safari rules state you must cross the finish line with your boat.

Just last year Phil and his team had to spend the night on a grassy island on the edge of the Victoria Barge Canal. Called "spoil islands" because they were formed from dredge sand during the canal excavation, they don't offer much in the way of protection from the elements. To stay warm Phil's team balled up like roly-poly bugs and leaned against each other's knees in a human chain.

I was a little bummed that we'd pull into Seadrift in the middle of the night. That meant that Sophie and my mom probably wouldn't be there. But my desire to reach the finish line and join them at the motel in my own clean, dry bed trumped all of my reservations.

There were houses and fishing cabins on stilts lining the river but we didn't see people in any of them. I had felt so good leaving the Saltwater Barrier after my rest and stretch session, but it didn't take long for the pain to settle back in. Phil could tell my paddling form wasn't top notch.

"Are you okay up there?"

"Yeah, my shoulders hurt. And my left elbow is giving me trouble."

"You know I'm really gonna need you full strength in the bay. Are you up for it?"

"I can do it. I'm good."

As pitiful as I felt, I knew I would rise to the occasion once we reached the bay. I just couldn't muster the intensity for this placid stretch of river.

"It's okay to conserve a little now. Because, seriously, the bay is no joke. We are both going to have to paddle as strong as we can to keep this boat upright. It's fast but it's just not as stable as others."

We paddled in silence as the sun slipped away and darkness enveloped us.

*Wow...my last day in the Texas Water Safari. I won't see the sun again on this race...*

I wiggled in my seat to try and relieve the pain in my butt.

My left shoulder was killing me and Phil hadn't called a "hut" in a while? I needed to switch. Dutifully I paddled on the same painful side for what seemed like an eternity. Finally he called it.

"Oh thank heavens." I groaned.

"Sorry. I'm getting a little tired. Spaced on that one. Feel free to call a hut if you need, especially when the water is this gentle and steering is pretty straightforward."

"No problem. How many times do you think you've said "hut" during this race?"

We both laughed. "Too many to count at this point, that's for sure."

"Are you still excited about your food order?"

"Oh yeah. I can't wait to eat normal food. What about you?"

"I can't wait either. I'm so excited for a big pile of pasta. What are you gonna do this week to recover?"

"Paddle."

"Oh come on?!"

"Seriously, I'm supposed to teach a paddling clinic later this week. Wanna help me?"

"Hell no! I am giving these shoulders a break."

"What are you gonna do?"

"I'll lie in bed in the A/C and watch movies for a few days, and then we head out to Montana. I am so excited to get out there and be on a river looking for fish. I used to think that rowing a drift boat for 8 or 9 miles in one day was huge. Not anymore."

At about 9 p.m. we paddled under the Tivoli Bridge and Highway 35. There were no spectators. No cowbells. No signs. We were alone, again, which often made it hard to remember that this was a race and not just an expedition.

My shoulders were starting to give out. My brain was sending the orders to rotate, but they were having no part of it.

Around 10 p.m. we rounded a small bend and approached a house on the left. It gave me pause because it looked so different than all the other wooden houses on stilts with the occasional screened porch. This house was stucco and faced the river sort of diagonally. The entire side of the house that was facing me was covered in spray-painted murals. How did I miss this in training? In broad daylight this certainly would have stood out. It looked like a graffiti-covered building in a major urban city. The murals were beautiful. I wondered if a group of kids had painted them.

But then, as we got closer, the house faded away and became a grove of liveoak trees. There were no murals. There wasn't even a house.

"Hey Phil..."

"Yup."

"My hallucinations are back."

"Mine too. I just saw a rhinoceros."

We tried to keep the conversation level up in hopes of stemming the odd visions, but each time there was a lull, my mind would begin fabricating weird paper mache shapes in the surrounding foliage. The gusting wind was whipping the tops of the trees, which only added to the surreal effects.

I tried to recall how many hours we had actually slept since the race started, but my weary mind couldn't come up with a number. Obviously, it wasn't nearly enough.

Phil called a "hut" and then added, "I really don't remember this part of the river very well from last year."

"I'm recognizing most of this from our training run back in May. The main thing is we *do not* want to take Traylor Cut."

"Where is that again?"

"Maybe halfway down to the mouth of the bay. Maybe a little more. It's tricky because the bulk of the river veers off to the left, which is actually Traylor Cut. It looks like that's the main river channel, but it's not."

"Is it like a sharp turn?"

"No. It's just that most of the water eases left and only a teeny narrow chute keeps on going straight. The cut looks like the river and the river looks like the cut. We want to go straight. Basically, when in doubt just hug the right bank."

Traylor Cut was bad news. It peels off from the Guadalupe and heads northeast (the wrong direction from Seadrift) and dumps into a large body of water called Mission Lake. Mission Lake is probably 2.5 by 1.5 miles and easily disorients weary paddlers. Even if a stray Safari boat reached Mission Lake and could navigate its way out, the two options were both pretty grim. One could backtrack upstream in Traylor Cut to return to the main river, but this would mean paddling against the current for quite a distance. The other option is crossing Mission Bay to the south where it eventually connects to Guadalupe and San Antonio Bay, but this also adds miles and miles of extra paddling.

Traylor Cut is to be avoided at all cost.

By 9:30 p.m. it was pitch black—no moon—and I was really fading. My spleen was sleepy. My toenails were sleepy. My throat was sleepy. I considered having a snack and putting some calories into my body but I was too tired to chew. I needed to talk.

"Phil, where do you want to put our spray skirt on? And our life vests?"

Water Safari rules required that every team must cross the bay with flares, a Coast Guard approved whistle, a Coast Guard approved white light (our bow light qualified), and life vests actually on your body. Spray skirts were not required by race officials but most boats used them. Some people created homemade spray skirts with Hefty bags and duct tape. Most people had a spray skirt made to fit their boat with some sort of nylon-coated lightweight fabric.

The spray skirt was critical to keep waves in the bay from swamping a boat, especially a low profile boat such as ours—and especially in the winds that we were about to experience.

Ours snapped around the edges of the boat, leaving two holes for each paddler to wiggle into their seat. Then the nylon material was pulled up below the armpits, and straps looped over your shoulders like overalls. For us, the spray skirt would be critical, but not ideal to paddle in if it wasn't needed. If we tumped, it would be very difficult to get back into the boat with the spray skirt affixed. It's really best to get into the spray skirt on solid land, or at least next to a bank where you can hold on for support.

Phil responded, "Well, that's a decision we need to make. There are few places along the river canal where it's safe to pull over and put the spray skirt on. There's a boat ramp that's public access on the left, if we didn't already pass it. Most people wait and do it at the grassy point at the mouth of the bay. That's what I suggest we do."

I remembered the grassy point from training. It was a clean, dry spit of land at the very point where the Guadalupe poured into the bay.

"Sounds good to me. Let's do it right before the bay."

Suddenly I remembered Traylor Cut.

*Where was it? Don't tell me we missed it. Impossible.*

I knew exactly what it looked like, I could picture it clearly in my mind. I was mortified at the thought of screwing up my main assignment on this leg of the race. I opened my eyes as wide as I could and focused intently. I wasn't going to miss it.

*Have we already missed it? No! That's crazy. There's no way.*

There hadn't been any opportunity to make a choice in any direction. We've just been traveling down a dark watery hallway.

At about 9:45 p.m. we finally found it.

"There it is, Phil. Just keep us to the right."

I felt much better. No more decisions to make, just straightforward paddling from there to the mouth of the bay.

After we passed Traylor Cut the Guadalupe became even tighter. I felt like a hamster in a Habitrail. The trees crowded in on us. The vegetation was lush and thick, almost like a jungle. It had looked exotic enough when I trained this section during the daytime, but at night it was beyond eerie. At points the trees curved over our heads, creating a true tunnel, and it was hard to see through to the sky.

Around 10:00 p.m. we reached the wooden bridge, which is the last public access spot. Supposedly this was a popular place for spectators, but apparently not on this night.

At the point where the river made its last hard turn to the left before its final two-mile run to the bay, we passed two people standing near some sort of pavilion. I wasn't lucid enough at the time to make note of what the building was exactly. I just assumed it was a covered party area or a carport for a river house, except there was no house nearby. At first I thought they may have been the property owners just hanging out next to the river, but then I saw their headlamps. They were racers.

As we paddled by silently we could make out a man and a young woman standing near the structure. They were staring at us and we were staring at them. I'm not sure which of us were the zoo animals and which of us were the humans, but we were locked in curiosity with each other.

We didn't wave or offer pleasantries. Nor did they.

The oddity of that encounter was just enough to keep me alert and awake for another minute or so. After the pavilion we were in our final stretch of river before the bay. I needed to be on point, but I was really feeling woozy. After another twenty minutes or so of paddling, I began nodding off as the boat created the same soporific effect of being in a rocking chair. I thought about the one at my parent's house in Montana. I would rock Sophie to sleep in that chair singing Loretta Lynn's "Love Is A Foundation" until we both dozed off.

As we continued paddling, I noticed a more distinct undulating sensation. I looked down at the water and tried to register what I was seeing. We were still paddling downriver, and yet it looked like the surface of the water was shifting back toward us. I blinked my eyes several times and kept staring.

"Phil?"

He sounded bewildered, "Yeah?"

"Do you see these little ripples coming at us?"

"Yeah…what the hell?"

As we spoke, they grew more pronounced.

He said, "This is crazy…."

One inch ripples quickly turned into two inches.

Almost immediately we were rocking over six-inch wave crests coming at us in a regular rhythm. I looked up at the overhanging tree canopy and noticed the upper branches whipping about. We were sheltered from the wind, which was blowing over our right shoulder from the southeast, so why are these waves coming toward us upriver? I wondered if maybe it was an incoming tide, but I didn't think we were that close to the bay.

I was wrong.

Within seconds we were bouncing through a one-foot chop. The bow of the boat would ascend each crest and then slide down the other side, then back up and down again.

"Phil, they're getting bigger."

"Just hold on. Keep paddling. Don't stop paddling!"

I was looking around for a spot to pull over, but both banks were thick with trees and brush.

Phil yelled, "Shit, we're at the bay…look at these rollers!"

The waves were over two feet high as we neared the end of the river channel. The wind hit us on our right beam and I paddled hard, knowing full well that if I stopped we might lose our balance and tip over.

"Dammit, where is that grassy point?"

There was no moon and our headlamps couldn't penetrate the blackness. We spotted a mesquite tree hanging over the right bank as we began losing control of the boat.

Phil yelled, "I'm getting out! Try and brace with your paddle."

I placed the flat paddle blade against the surface but it did little to hold us steady as the bow rose and fell with the waves. When Phil jumped out the stern spun around to the left. Our 24-foot boat was now diagonal to the current and waves, practically stretching across the width of the river mouth.

Phil held on to one of the tree branches and tried to tie the bow rope to the tree. That was taking too long. "Listen," he yelled over the roar of the wind. "We need to get on our life vests right away. And we need to try and keep this boat from sinking. And then we need to find that grassy spot."

"Okay."

"I need you to get out of the boat, hold onto the tree, and hold the bow line while I get the life vests out."

"Okay."

I jumped out on the right side of the boat and swam to the tree. I grabbed a thin branch but it snapped off in my hand. I grabbed another, it snapped off. I dog-paddled in the water and kept reaching until I found a branch strong enough to hold onto.

"Got it!"

"Alright, here's the bow line. Don't lose it or the boat could sink."

I grabbed the bowline and wrapped it around my right hand, which was holding the tree branch. I tried to steady the bow of the canoe with my left hand, but the waves were lifting it way over my head and then slamming it back down.

Phil fished out the life vests and managed to push mine toward me through the tree branches. I now had my life vest in my left hand and the bowline and tree branch in my right, while floating up to my armpits in the middle of a gale. I need to get my life vest on, but this wasn't going to work. I needed another hand.

"Phil, can you hold the bow line while I do this?"

"Sure, work it through here."

I threaded the bow line through some branches over to Phil. Still holding on to the tree I was able to unlock the buckles on the life vest with my left hand, but I couldn't open it up and get my arm into it without my right hand helping. Finally, I found a submerged branch that I could brace against, so I let go with my right hand and rolled over on my back in the water. It took some doing, but I finally got both arms into the vest and buckled it tight.

Then it was Phil's turn. He handed the bow rope back to me and executed some similar acrobatic move in the water to get his vest on. We were clinging to that tree like wet little koala bears, trying to figure out our next move when we both noticed a light coming from upriver. We looked at each other and without saying a word, agreed to wait and see what happened.

Their bow was rocking up and down on the waves as they paddled toward us. It was a dad and his teenage daughter. They managed to pull off to the right, just upriver from us, without tumping.

"Are y'all alright?" the dad yelled.

"Yeah," Phil answered. "These waves are huge. Be careful!"

Still hugging the tree, I yelled out, "We're trying to get to that grassy point at the mouth of the bay. Do you know if we're close?"

The man looked at me funny, but then politely pointed over my head. "It's right there, behind that tree you're on."

I turned and looked over my shoulder.

*Now, where did that come from?*

I released my white-knuckle death grip and swam a few feet past the tree. My toes immediately found the bottom and I pulled myself out on the grassy point.

"Are you kidding me? We were here all along?"

Phil and I hauled our boat up onto the point and they did the same. We could barely hear ourselves over the wind.

"I'm Gary, this is my daughter Kristin," the dad yelled.

"I'm Christine, and this is Phil Meyer."

We all had a good laugh. I told the guy, "Don't worry. If you're wondering whether or not you should tell people the story about running into two dimwits clinging to a tree for dear life without a clue that they were about a foot from safety…I promise I'll tell it first."

Even though we were in a safe spot, the grassy point wasn't nearly as dry and inviting as I'd remembered. The incoming waves had covered it with about six inches of water.

It was about 11 p.m. None of us really knew what to do. From our limited vantage of the bay we could plainly see it was incredibly rough. The waves looked like white frosting tips whipped up on a huge muddy cake. We sloshed around in the marshy grass for a bit, scratching our heads and discussing the bay. It made me realize how out of touch we'd been with the world.

"Is this a storm or some sort of front?" I asked.

Phil sounded tired, "I have no clue."

Of course he didn't. How would he know? He'd been sequestered with me all these days and hours, equally out of sync with the pulse of everyday life.

"It looks pretty bad out there," he said.

We heard more voices from the river channel. We gathered around the edge and watched as Jamie and Brian came bouncing toward us into the waves. They, too, managed to navigate a secure spot against the bank, infinitely more effectively than we had. They were scrambling up the bank with their boat just as Max and Mike paddled up. The high flared bow of their aluminum canoe was really bouncing as they approached.

Max and Mike joined the party and we all cussed this stroke of bum luck. A nasty, blown out bay. Who could have seen this coming? We would later learn that there was no storm. These straight line winds from the southeast are well known on the Texas Coast and they can come at any time of the year.

Once the adrenalin wore off from the fear and excitement, reality took hold of me. We weren't crossing the bay that night, or maybe anytime soon. My heart sank. I looked wistfully into the black sky hanging over the bay while the wind roared over my shoulder, batting my braid about like a cat with a play toy. I dug out a Clif bar and sipped on my water tube. Phil found a snack of his own.

I'd been desperate to get my bottom out of that seat for over a day but for some reason I had an overwhelming urge to sit down. There was too much standing water to sit on the ground. I tried sitting in my seat in the boat but it was too tippy.

The eight of us kicked ideas around for a while before reaching the obvious consensus. The bay was way too rough and we should get some sleep. We started tromping around the point looking for a mildly dry place to sleep. We covered over a hundred yards in various directions but couldn't find a place with less than five inches of water.

Mike climbed into their aluminum canoe and curled up in his seat. Their boat had higher sides and was more stable. Max confirmed, "I think we're gonna sleep here in our boat."

The rest of us caucused about the best plan. Phil offered, "I'd say it's best to sleep in the boat but we can't. We don't have room in ours. Plus it's too tippy."

Jamie seemed uncertain.

Gary offered another option. "Do y'all know about the Holiday Inn?"

I shook my head no, but hoped it came with continental breakfast.

"It's that pavilion where we were when y'all passed us earlier," Gary explained.

"Oh, that was *y'all*?"

"Yeah, we were watching you guys and wondering if you were really gonna go for it in this wind. When you kept paddling, we decided we would try it too."

"What's the deal with that pavilion?" I asked.

"Well, it's on private property but the owner is Safari-friendly. It's a known deal that racers can stop there to put on spray skirts, or spend the night. That's why a lot of racers call it the Holiday Inn."

Jamie asked, "How far back upriver is it?"

I cringed at the very notion of paddling back upstream. I did not like to backtrack. I was all about advancing.

Gary answered, "Maybe like two miles."

There was a collective groan.

Jamie added, "The winds will be the most calm right before dawn. I think I'd like to be here to jump on it if they let up at all."

Phil nodded. "That's true. If we could just sleep in our boat, we'd be in business." He looked at me for input.

I wasn't excited about it but offered to sleep on the wet grass.

No one really saw that as a viable option.

Gary continued about the Holiday Inn, "There's also a road there. By morning there'll be Safari volunteers and team captains that show up. They might come looking for us there when we don't show up in Seadrift tonight. Could be good if we have to wait this wind out for awhile tomorrow and need more water."

It was a tough call. Paddling back upstream seemed like absolute torture. Not to mention it would add more mileage in the morning before we could get a jump on the bay. Then again, some decent sleep on dry ground would probably do wonders for our bodies on this bay crossing, whenever it happened.

Phil opted for heading back to the Holiday Inn but left the decision to me. There was no clear answer so I called it. Holiday Inn.

Brian, Jamie, Gary and Kristin were still mulling it over while we set our plan into motion. I told Phil, "If we're going, then let's go now. No sense getting more tired here, let's get all the rest we can so we're ready when the wind lies down."

He agreed.

As we were preparing to shove off and head back upriver, I looked down and noticed the blinking light on our SPOT Tracker. I had completely forgotten about it. The Safari allowed SPOT trackers because the signal they send out is one-way communication, not two-way. Basically every so often it would update our exact GPS location and place a red dot on a map on a dedicated website that showed our progress. I had sent the link to friends and family thinking it would be fun for them to follow along, but no one really said anything about it before the race. Oh well, at least it had been useful for our team captain and chase team to follow our progress between checkpoints.

It was midnight when we loaded our boat into the water, said our farewells and began our retreat. I had to laugh at the image of us on the SPOT Tracker. A little red dot heading back upriver. "Hey Phil, what if Banning, or Tosh, or someone who really knows this course is watching right now? Can you imagine what they're thinking?"

For the first quarter mile we rode the waves back up the Guadalupe like surfers. Once they leveled off it was nothing more than a grueling, but thankfully short, paddle back upriver.

About halfway to the pavilion I noticed a burning, itching sensation on my left thigh. I stopped paddling to scratch and Phil noticed.

"What's up?"

"Something must have bit me, my leg is on fire…"

I scratched and scratched but of course that just made it worse. Then the top of my right thigh started burning."

"Phil my legs are making me crazy, I wonder if I've got poison ivy?"

"Probably. No telling what we walked through on that logjam portage."

It was agony. The dangling commitment I still felt to my partner to keep paddling was the only thing that prevented me from clawing at my legs like a flea-bit dog.

We reached the boat ramp and the pavilion at around 1 a.m. We were physically destroyed and still mentally reeling from the close call in the waves at the river mouth. We couldn't drag the canoe up the concrete ramp without damaging it, so we each lifted an end and hauled it out onto the grass. The poison ivy was driving me crazy and I wondered if the oils from that evil plant had soaked into my clothes.

"Phil, don't look. I'm stripping down to take a bath in the river. I have to do something to help this poison ivy."

I took off my shirt, shorts, and tights. With my headlamp I could see a red splotchy rash all over my thighs. I walked down to the river in nothing but my sports bra, panties, shoes and headlamp and jumped into the dark, muddy water. I dunked down to my neck and used the palm of my hand as a washcloth. I don't think I did anything to improve my hygiene issues but at least I was tricking my mind into thinking I was doing something to help the poison ivy.

Phil was organizing his gear and politely looking the other way as I walked back up the ramp to grab my spare tights and shorts from their Seal-a-meal packs. No reason to save them, now. It felt great to be out of the nasty, muddy stuff that I'd been wearing since Saturday.

Instead of putting my wet shirt back on, I laid it out to dry and put on my lightweight rain jacket, instead. Since we would actually have time for a proper nap, I cut into the packet that housed my space blanket, a paper thin silver mylar sheet that folds up into the size of nothing and is supposed to conserve body heat. I wasn't taking any chances with chills. I wanted some actual sleep before we tackled the bay in the morning.

We walked over to the concrete pad that was covered with a tin roof.

"You can take the bench," Phil offered.

"No, you go ahead. I really wouldn't be comfortable on that. I'll stretch out on the floor."

I laid out my foam pad and my life vest pillow and took off my shoes. My feet were a strange day glo white and looked like those nasty pickled pig's feet that you see in jars in country convenience stores. Why did pigs feet always look so plump floating in that liquid? Mine had been in liquid for three days and were completely wrinkled and unrecognizable. I tried rubbing them and layers of skin sloughed off in my hand.

Mosquitoes swarmed my headlamp so I clicked it off and set it next to my makeshift bed. As I pulled the mylar sheet over me I settled into my spot on the concrete. It was as hard and unforgiving as you might imagine, but so much smoother than anything my body had touched in the past three days. It was strange to reconnect with something so clearly manmade.

As we settled down to rest we heard voices coming up to the boat ramp. We sat up and looked down. It was Gary and Kristin. We waited a little while until they unloaded from their boat and made their way over to the concrete pad.

"So y'all decided to paddle back?" I asked, stating the obvious.

"Yeah." Gary answered while Kristin nodded with droopy eyes.

That's about all any of us could muster. Gary and Kristin stretched out a few feet away from me. When I last checked my watch it was about 2 a.m. We would get at least four hours of sleep before daylight, which would be like winning the lottery. We'd wake up at first light and the wind would be calm and we'd finally get our shot to cross the bay.

I figured my mom and Sophie had bedded down hours ago. They were none the wiser about this heartbreaking delay. But I couldn't help but wonder what my dad, Tom, and Monica were thinking when we hadn't showed up in Seadrift.

I closed my eyes with the wind still howling, and my legs itching like crazy.

# CHAPTER 24

# GUADALUPE BAY TO FINISH

*"Launch yourself on every wave, find your eternity*
*in each moment."*
–HENRY DAVID THOREAU

I'm not sure how long I slept. After three days of intense physical output and sleep deprivation, I should have slept like a baby, or even better, a teenager until noon. Sadly, that was not the case.

I got cold again and the mylar blanket wasn't getting the job done. Shivering, I curled up tight into a little ball trying to create warmth. Every time I moved or rolled over, the mylar blanket would crinkle and crackle. More than once I woke to find my hand violently scratching my calf. Dammit, it was spreading. I scratched so much that I inadvertently ripped the mylar Space Blanket into shreds. Frustrated, I whipped the useless thing off of me and tossed it aside.

Turns out the concrete wasn't the best place to bed down. Granted it was clean and dry, but since it was shaded during the day, it hadn't absorbed heat like those wonderful toasty gravel bars that I was used to. I thought about moving over to the grass, but didn't want to expend the energy.

I drifted in and out for a few hours, at one point maybe logging forty five minutes without waking up. Unfortunately the mosquitoes got word that I was actually content and flocked over to make certain that it wouldn't last. I woke up to them buzzing around my ears, my lips and up my nose. I swear they were even attracted to the wetness of my eyeballs.

As I squeezed my eyes shut to keep the tiny vampires out, I had a lightbulb moment. Something I'd experienced dozens of times on the water.

*Mosquitoes don't like wind, so if they're this bad, then the wind must have died!*

In my groggy dream state I fully convinced myself that tomorrow morning we'd be paddling across a glassy smooth bay to the finish line. Still curled up on my side, I popped my eyes open to see my premonition firsthand.

The palm trees were still dipping and bending and shaking their heads as if to say, *Sorry. We're not happy about this either.*

I lay there for a while longer, bummed about the wind, scratching my legs and blowing mosquitoes out of my mouth. At about 5:45, I'd had enough. There was faint color in the eastern sky and it was time to get moving. Phil was awake too, so we tiptoed past Gary and Kristin and met near the canoe.

Neither of us really leapt into go-mode. It was still darkish so I got my clothes and gear organized. My shirt and shorts were still soaking wet but I put them back on. There are few sensations more unappealing that putting on wet, clingy, dirty clothes. I tucked the rain jacket away, rolled up my foam pad, and clipped my life vest back onto the crossbar. Neither Phil nor I had much to say as we rifled through the remnants of our food and found snack bars. I was pretty grouchy by the time I sipped on my Cytomax. It was so disgusting to me at that point that I took it as a personal affront and felt the urge to hurl the water jugs against a tree trunk. If I thought for one second it would make my legs stop itching I would have done it. I cursed Phil under my breath for nixing that small tube of Benadryl gel. It had poison ivy leaves on the *flippin' label*, thank you very much. Team Paddlefish spirit was pretty low.

It was completely light at 6:30 when we heard a car coming down the road. Gary and Kristin looked over and the four of us watched a red SUV approach. Like castaways who had forgotten their native tongue, we stared with mouths agape as the four-wheeled machine from the outside world slowed down, and pulled in next to the pavilion.

Two women stepped out wearing Safari t-shirts and we literally mobbed them for information. We wanted to know what was going on with the bay. Was there a storm? What was the word from Seadrift? They had folding chairs and were setting up camp to wait for the woman's son, the girl's husband who was paddling solo. They were a wealth of information.

"The bay has been really ugly. Last we heard it was sustained at thirty and gusting to forty," the woman offered up. "There are probably ten or twelve people that have been stuck out on the spoil islands all night. They started out and it was simply too rough to go on, too rough to turn back. There's talk that a solo paddler is out there and is running out of food and water."

Phil wanted details. "Do you know who all's out there?"

She shook her head. "Not really. I know the Hippie Chicks are."

"Whoa!" I thought they would be in Seadrift long ago, showered and fresh as daisies by now. I followed up with, "What's going on with the weather? Does anyone in Seadrift have a prediction what the bay is going to do?"

She shook her head. "It doesn't look good. Basically Tom Goynes said about now is the only time it's going to be remotely calm. Then the wind is supposed to get stronger."

Tom Goynes is the unofficial godfather of the Texas Water Safari. He and his wife own a campground along the San Marcos River. He had raced many times through the years, as had his daughter and son-in-law. He offered the blessing at the beginning of the race and kept the time sheet at the finish line. Tom Goynes was well respected by all Safari factions and pretty much whatever he said was word.

I looked at Phil and thought, should we get going?

We listened to the rest of her report. "Erin Magee is out."

We were shocked. "Really?" Phil asked. "Are you serious? She's been training like a madwoman for months."

"Yeah, she made it past the Barrier but was hurting so badly by the wooden bridge, just upriver from here, that she had her team captain come and get her out."

That was depressing news. Only to be topped by the next nugget.

"And West and Katie are out."

"What?" we exclaimed in unison.

"Yeah, Katie quit at Cheapside and West actually paddled their boat alone to the next checkpoint, at Cuero. But then he got out there."

I felt nauseous. I hated hearing these reports. The giants were falling. My mentors were no longer in the race.

That reminded me, "Do you know anything about Eric Wilder and his partner Dan?"

She shook her head apologetically.

"What about Bugge?"

"Oh yeah," she said as if it were a silly question. "They finished yesterday morning."

I was happy to hear that. At least something in the world was working the way it was supposed to.

Then the tables turned and the two women had a question for us. "Have y'all seen Sam Hilker on the water at all?"

We nodded, curious why she was asking.

"Her team captain is worried about her. She didn't clock in at one of the checkpoints when they expected her. They still don't know where she is. Race officials are looking for her."

I was bummed and speechless.

Phil guessed that Sam's fiancé, Wade, had probably already finished the race and was on it. "What about Wade, where did he come in? He was on the six-man team with the Mynars."

"They came in second."

Phil was calm. "I'm sure she's okay."

I felt obliged to share what we knew in case these women ran into some of Sam's team. "We paddled with her off and on between Hochheim and Cuero. The last place we saw her was right above the Victoria Checkpoint. She had told us about her plan to deal with the logjams below Dupont. She was planning to take a cut into Alligator Lake to avoid the big logjam. But Wade was the one who told her that plan, so he already knows she was heading in there."

All of this dour news had a heavy effect on us. I couldn't believe all these Safari legends were out of the race. It was just as everyone said all along; no one was guaranteed a finish. But if *they* couldn't finish, what chance did *I* have?

The group dispersed and Phil approached me one on one. Calmly he laid it out for me. "Listen, with this wind, I don't think the bay is going to calm down for a long time. We've run an incredible race. You have basically come the whole way. You have so much to be proud of. There would be no shame in bowing out here. I have a Safari patch so you won't be letting me down at all. It's your call but I just want you to know we could be here a long time waiting this out. Or we could get out there and get stuck in the bay for a very long time."

I shuddered at the mention of quitting. I thought about Tom, my mom and dad and Sophie waiting for me at the finish line, ready to celebrate, not console. I thought about the Rett Syndrome families and all my friends that had contributed to their cause. I thought about Rancey and Ella and how I promised to speak for them. What would I be saying if I quit?

*I am NOT going to quit.*

We had plenty of food and water and we had banked a huge number of hours. At this point we weren't in any danger of a DNF based on time.

I looked at Phil, and simply stated, "I don't want to quit. If we press on to the bay, what's the worst that could happen?"

"We could get out there and tump, and if we can't get back into the spray skirt, we may have to swim or walk the boat a long way. Or we might have to stay on the spoil islands for another night."

"But we're good on food and water."

"Right."

"And we're both good swimmers."

"Yep."

"Can't you stand in most of the bay?"

"Yep, most of it's three to six feet. The barge canal is deep but we're not supposed to be in there anyway except to cross it quickly."

"Obviously I'm not minimizing how badly it would suck to have to swim or walk the boat. And spending the night on the spoil islands sounds pretty awful. But aside from the misery, none of that is really all that dangerous. Unless we pass out from fatigue, float into the barge canal and get run over."

"There's that."

"But really, considering the most likely of all situations, the worst case scenario is we tump, can't get back in, and it will take 12-20 hours to walk and swim the boat to the finish."

"Yep."

I thought about it all for a few moments.

"Well, Phil. Time is actually on our side. It's not even 7:00 a.m. on Tuesday. This race doesn't end until 1 p.m. Wednesday. We've paddled our asses off to get down here. We haven't sweated one cutoff time at one checkpoint. The way I see it we have over thirty hours to give this a shot. Plus, we have over twelve hours of daylight. It doesn't seem so bad in the daytime."

I couldn't believe those words had just came out of my mouth. For three days I had cursed the sun, but something about this bay crossing was different. I felt better tackling it with plenty of light.

Phil looked at me, smiled, and said, "Okay, let's do it."

It took a little while to get organized to make our final push. I was desperate for something to spread on my poison ivy and since it wasn't the time to whine about the fact that we hadn't brought the anti-itch gel, I would have to make do. I literally was willing to spread anything on my legs, so I grabbed one of my chocolate electrolyte gel packs.

*Chocolate makes everything better, right?*

I supposed spending three days and nights in such close quarters gave Phil some instinct about how my mind worked because he caught me just as I was about to do it.

"Christine…what are you doing?"

"I am putting this chocolate electrolyte goo on my poison ivy."

Approaching me with caution, he gestured with his hands for me to slow down. He spoke to me calmly like I was a crazy person wielding a gun or a grenade. "I…I don't think that's going to help."

"Anything! Anything will help. I need to put *something* on this rash. Wait…Desitin! What about *Desitin*?"

He shrugged.

"Where is it?" I demanded with my hand out. "Cough it up. I know you've got it hidden away someplace."

Begrudgingly he produced the final remnants of our communal Desitin tube. Even in my utter desperation I couldn't be so selfish. I decided to at least give him fair warning. "I am going to use every last ounce of this on my poison ivy. So speak now if you need any more of it. This is it."

He laughed. "Go ahead. It's all yours."

I turned my back to Phil, Gary and Kristin, reached into my tights and slathered a thick coating of Desitin all over my thighs and knees. I couldn't reach my calves, so this would have to do.

To top things off I figured a little ibuprofin couldn't hurt. Phil saw me going for the pills and I thought he was going to stop me.

"Actually that's probably a good idea. It will probably take the edge off the rash."

While I reveled in the fact that I had just dosed myself with a lethal Desitin-Motrin cocktail, Phil dug out his laminated map of the bay. We had reviewed it many times before, most recently during our quick break at the Barrier. But he wanted to discuss the options one more time.

Gary and Kristin wandered over. They had decided to go for it as well. Gary had completed the Safari several times; he and Kristin had finished it together just the year before. They prepared their boat while Phil and I discussed the direction of the wind and analyzed which path would be best for us.

Basically, when we reached the mouth of the river, the shortest route to Seadrift would be to peel off to the right and paddle on a diagonal path heading southeast across the bay. After four miles we'd hit Foster's Point at the tip of the spoil islands along the edge of the barge canal. From there it's about a two mile sprint, following the shoreline and seawall to the finish.

Phil thought that the wind direction could actually help us. It would be blowing toward the shoreline the entire way, so at least the wind would be pushing us toward Seadrift and not into the open bay.

That was mildly comforting.

But he was also concerned that the wind direction on the first leg would be bad for a tippy boat like ours. He suggested that instead of aiming for Foster's Point, which would require paddling through more rough water, that we shoot straight across to the spoil islands and then follow them down to Foster's. It added over half a mile to our route, but provided more time in sheltered water.

I voted for that route. Even though the spoil islands were

nothing more than wispy clumps of marsh grass, something about them comforted me. I liked the idea of having them beside us as opposed to spending so much time in open water.

"Okay, here's the deal," Phil said, "I'm pretty sure we're gonna tump and this could be a pretty wild ride. Be ready to go over. The thing is, once we tump we're probably swimming it and walking from there because there really isn't anyplace out there to get back in the boat with the spray skirt. Paddling is so much faster. The longer we stay upright paddling, the faster we get to Seadrift."

"Got it."

"I am really gonna need everything you've got out there."

"Got it. I'm ready."

Since we'd given Monica our daytime stuff at the Barrier, we had to pull out our spare sunglasses and hats. We unfurled the spray skirt and spread it out over the boat. We went around the edges snapping it into place. We put our life vests back on. Patiently, Phil held the boat steady in the shallow water on the boat ramp while I stuffed myself into my seat through the hole in the spray skirt. I found the straps and fastened them over my shoulders.

Phil then worked his way into his spot. Gary and Kristin seemed ready to go as well. The sun was bright in the sky, and our spirits were high. It was about 7 a.m. as we paddled away from the Holiday Inn.

Phil asked me, "Do you know how to get out of that spray skirt if we tump?"

"Uh…no."

"If we go upside down, you obviously don't want those straps holding you in place under water.

Yep, that sounded awful.

"So basically, the minute we go over, push those straps off your shoulders and start kicking as hard as you can. Once you are up and safe, it's pretty important to locate your paddle and the boat as quickly as possible. But most important is straps down, kick like hell until you are out of the spray skirt."

I didn't say anything, but that freaked me out.

*Why were we just now covering this lesson?*

Of all the hours we'd noodled over where to tape down the bow light wires, how many Zip-ties to bring, how to choreograph each portage, I couldn't believe we forgot to discuss this little doozie scenario. Lord knows we'd had countless hours of silent paddling desperate for a conversation topic.

Phil called out. "The waves are starting."

I mentally rehearsed his instructions. I wasn't sure I had it down.

*What was it again? Straps down and kick kick kick. Okay, I was ready. Straps down and kick kick kick.*

The two miles back to the bay passed quickly. Soon it was obvious that the wind had not died much during the night. Little did we know that it would get worse before getting any better.

As we approached the mouth of the river, the waves were rolling in just as big as the night before. Max and Mike and Jamie and Brian were nowhere to be seen. Obviously they had already started their push for the finish.

Phil shouted up at me, "We can't hit the bay slowly or it will flip us right out of the gate. We need speed to create stability. So when I say so, paddle with everything you've got."

I nodded firmly so he could see my agreement from the stern.

When we reached the mouth, Phil turned to Gary and Kristin next to us, "Y'all are going straight for Foster's Point so why don't y'all take the lead."

Gary nodded and they paddled ahead of us. It was about 7:30 a.m. when we reached the end of the Guadalupe River. I watched in awe as Gary and Kristin buckled down and flew out of the chute. The minute they hit the bay they cut to the right and burrowed southeast toward Foster's Point. Their paddle strokes were fast and in sync.

Phil shouted, "Okay, this is it. Ready?"

I nodded emphatically.

We used every bit of runway we had at the end of the river channel to get up speed and burst into the bay at full force.

"Paddle! Paddle! Paddle hard!"

It was exhilarating. I kept my eyes locked straight ahead at the muddy waves right in front of the bow. But in my peripheral vision I couldn't help but notice what was on my left and on my right: nothing. Nothing but wide-open space. Open water. After being nestled in the corridor of the river for three days and nights it was surreal to be out in this bright airy space.

I suddenly had a pang of nostalgia for the river. We'd traveled all this way together and *poof*, just like that, the river was gone. Its journey was complete just six miles shy of ours. The river had taken us so far; I suppose I had forgotten that it wouldn't be with us for the final stretch.

I paddled with every bit of power I could muster. Every muscle in my body was pushing us forward. I no longer felt my shoulders, my back or my aching butt. Even the itch had subsided.

Adrenaline is an extraordinary thing.

Our strokes were fast. When the blades were in the water, we were stable. When they left the water we were vulnerable. I returned to my best paddling form, abs engaged, back straight, full rotation. I tried to make each stroke count, grabbing water and pulling the boat forward.

The waves were unbelievable. They were coming at us from the right, almost perpendicular to the boat. That's pretty much worst-case scenario, ideally you want to tackle waves head on. But we were making a run for the spoil islands, hoping for relief once we got there. Unlike the large rolling waves we'd experienced inside the river mouth, these packed more of a punch. We fought like hell to keep forward motion, which was our only chance to stay upright.

*Breathe. Breathe. Don't be too tense. Remember what Bugge said, loose hips. Don't be rigid. Move with the boat, not against it.*

I conjured images of the Pilates training I'd done. I tried to exude that perfect mix of power and fluidity. Strong and supple.

I allowed myself to sneak a peek ahead and was overcome with joy. We were making progress. The spoil islands were getting closer. But the waves were still huge and I couldn't relax. I was beginning to worry about making the sharp turn to the right once we reached the islands. I sensed we were a precariously balanced house of cards. Any alteration could topple the whole deal.

Apparently my concern was legitimate. As we grew closer Phil announced, "Hang on. I am gonna start turning us right. Just keep paddling. Don't stop paddling!"

"Hut!"

Slowly the bow came around to the right, and miraculously we were still upright, paddling southeast, now, with the islands along our left.

Phil yelled, "I have my foot pushing down as hard as I can on the right pedal just to keep us straight. The wind is pushing us into the islands. I need you to keep paddling on the left. Are you okay not switching?"

"I'm good. I got it!"

Now the waves were coming at us head on which was easier. I started to see the pattern. Big wave, small, small, small. Big wave, small, small, small. I took deep breaths to keep my balance. I paddled as hard as possible.

Phil added, "If you are at the top of a wave and your paddle goes into the trough, catching air, that's okay, just keep the rhythm. Paddle hard."

I kept the pace on the left side while Phil paddled in sync and leaned all of his weight onto the pedal. The rudder on our boat was being taxed to its limit.

Phil yelled over the wind, "Do you have a puddle forming in the spray skirt up there?"

I looked at where my knees should be. Extra fabric was sitting low as water was collecting in a pool of the fabric.

"Yes!"

"I can feel it back here. It's throwing us off balance. If we collect too much water it could swamp us. Can you bail it out?"

I nodded and used my hand to grab the fabric and pop the water over the right side of the boat.

"Whoa! Whoa! You need to let me know when you're gonna do it. I have to have my paddle in the water the moment you do to help keep us stable. Try and read the pattern of the waves. Do it in between the smaller ones and call it out first."

"Okay."

I noted the pattern of the waves. Big wave, small, small, small. Big wave, small, small, small. Water was collecting again.

"Bailing!"

"Go!"

I grabbed a fistful of fabric, popped the excess water over the right side and resumed paddling as quickly as possible.

This was intense. And euphoric.

Up ahead we saw Jamie and Brian walking their boat through the muddy waves. I was too nervous to turn my head and say "hi" for fear it would shift my weight and tump us, but I gave a mini cheer as we paddled by them. Out of the corner of my eye I saw them wave us on.

We continued in this rhythm toward Foster's Point. Up and over waves. Bailing the spray skirt. Paddling vigorously. Through the openings between the islands we could see the barge canal running parallel on the opposite side.

"We're doing great!" Phil yelled.

I nodded and kept after it. As we neared Foster's Point the waves grew more and more intense. Again I recognized that making the turn to the left around the point was going to be tricky. Waves were crashing into each other at the point causing all sorts of turbulence.

*Straps down and kick kick kick!*

We paddled hard and actually cleared the point. But the waves were huge and flailing in all directions. As soon as we hit them we tumped.

*Straps down and kick kick kick!*

Truthfully, I slid right out with very little effort. The water was only about waist deep and my feet quickly found the bottom. I was still clutching my paddle.

"Whoo hoo!" Phil shouted. "That was awesome!"

I didn't know much, but I knew we had just far exceeded expectations. We had clearly paddled farther than Phil thought we'd be able to. I was giddy thinking about the hours we shaved off by paddling further and walking less.

Now that we were on foot with the waves crashing into us and the boat, I started to understand why it would be such a pain to have to walk it all the way in. Phil led us back toward the point. Amazingly enough we tucked around the east side facing the barge canal and were somewhat protected from the wind and waves.

We laughed and high-fived, relishing our accomplishment. Phil said, "Let's have some water and a snack. We just burned a ton of calories."

He dug around inside the spray skirt blindly with his hands like reaching into a grab bag at the fair. He found snacks from his stash and handed me one of his mini Payday candy bars. Then he fished one of the drinking tubes out from beneath the spray skirt, and we both took a long drink.

Phil outlined our next steps. "Here's the deal. This is the barge canal. It's deep so we'll have to swim the boat straight across.

Then we're at the mainland. We have to get around one tricky pier that seems to cause people trouble, but after that we're at the seawall."

I knew this part. "From the pier to the finish line is about 2,000 feet. Piece of cake."

"Yep."

We relaxed a second longer, just long enough for Phil to have another idea.

"It's calm here and we can hold the boat steady. Do you want to try and get back into the spray skirt so we can paddle?"

"Sure. What have we got to lose?"

Phil straddled the bow of the boat, stabilizing it as best he could with his legs on each side. Carefully I tucked one foot into the hole in the spray skirt that was near my seat. I held the sides of the boat, trying to apply equal pressure to both sides so as not to flip it. I then lifted my right leg into the spray skirt hole and wiggled into my seat. From there I pulled up the straps and fastened them back on my shoulders.

"Oh my gosh, I'm in!"

"Now, here's the real test. I don't know how I am going to do this."

As I had done before, I placed the blade of my paddle flat on the surface to help keep us balanced. I don't know what Cirque du Soleil move he did back there but the boat stopped jiggling and Phil yelled out, "I'm in."

I laughed out loud. "I can't believe this, we're paddling again!"

The barge canal was the smoothest water we would see in the bay. It was a shame we couldn't just slice down the middle of it. But I suppose Safari officials had our safety in mind when they ruled we could only cut straight across.

With that, I did look left and right just to make sure I hadn't overlooked something charging our way.

We aimed straight across and then angled toward Seadrift. As we moved away from the barge canal and back into open water, the waves returned. I set aside the celebratory thoughts and refocused. We use the same routine as before for another mile or so. Paddling hard, breathing into the waves, monitoring their patterns. I noticed I was having to bail the spray skirt more frequently. The waves were getting bigger. I couldn't believe we were still upright.

Phil was excited. "That big pier is the beginning of the seawall. That's it. From there we can literally walk it down the seawall if we want. We're in the home stretch."

I was excited but focused. The waves were growing bigger and stronger. I felt if I took my eyes off of them it would throw off our timing and we'd be back in the water. When we reached the pier, Phil angled us out away from it to give us plenty of clearance. When we got even with the seawall the waves were smashing against it and bouncing back toward us with a lot of turbulence.

"Keep paddling! Give me everything you've got, they're getting bigger!"

The wind was howling and we were losing our voices trying to communicate with each other.

Phil shouted, "There's Tom and your dad!"

I quickly turned and saw them, and then re-focused on my paddling. They were near the pier huddled by a car. I guess they drove down to look for us.

They went nuts when they saw us. They were shouting, cheering and screaming. I couldn't look over and wave but I smiled and kept peeking over out of the corner of my left eye. I could tell they were scrambling to get in their car and drive back down to the finish line.

Phil was elated, "This is it. We're practically there. It's a done deal."

My heart soared. It was overwhelming. Two-thousand feet came out to about .38 miles out of 260 miles total.

*Yeah, we've got this!*

Phil explained, "I'm sorry I'm keeping us so far off the seawall. The waves are crashing off the wall so hard, it's just too rough over there. I'm going to keep us out here as long as we can keep paddling."

My family re-appeared on the seawall near the finish and were cheering us in. As we began to angle toward the steps at the finish line, our bow started dipping and heaving between the peaks and troughs. We pushed on as far as we could, but about a hundred feet shy of the steps, we tumped.

The crowd went crazy cheering for us. We sprang to our feet in waist deep water and I waved at my family, pumping my paddle into the air. I imagine the grin on my face was pretty silly.

As we walked the boat in our team gathered at the steps. Monica was at the top of the steps with my family and Tim Cole. Cameras were clicking left and right. It's tradition for earlier finishers to be there at the steps to hoist your boat up for you. John Bugge was among a group of fellow racers waiting for us, and they pulled the Team Paddlefish boat out of the water and up the steps. Phil and I held onto the rails and climbed the steps side by side.

At precisely 10:21 a.m. on Tuesday, July 13, 2010, Team Paddlefish completed the 48th running of the Texas Water Safari.

Sophie was standing off to the right with the biggest smile I'd ever seen. I peeled off to hug her but the crowd shouted at me, "Go under! Go under!"

I turned and walked back under the crude wooden sign with "Texas Water Safari" spelled out in wooden block letters, and practically fell into Tom and Sophie's arms. Never, in my entire life, has a hug felt better or meant more.

I could see my mom and dad tearing up. Sophie was wrapped around my waist and Tom was hugging me tight around my shoulders. Tears filled his eyes as he congratulated me. It was a raw and poetic moment and I was overwhelmed with joy. I hugged my mom, and then my dad. I was so happy they were both there. Next came Monica, our rock, who had kept us organized, fueled and moving forward. As everyone scrambled to line up for photos beneath the Texas Water Safari sign, Phil turned to me with his hand in the air for a high-five and said, "Nice work partner, we did it!"

Yes, we did.

## Seadrift Checkpoint

| | |
|---|---|
| CUTOFF TIME: | WEDNESDAY 1:00 P.M. |
| OUR TIME: | TUESDAY 10:21 A.M. |
| PLACE: | 39TH |
| TIME ELAPSED: | 73 HOURS AND 21 MINUTES |
| MILES PADDLED: | 260 |
| MILES TO GO: | 0 |

# CHAPTER 25

# SEADRIFT

*"Thank you for remembering me. I'm also happy to be accepting this trophy before I become incontinent."*

-BILL COSBY

The finish line was bustling with activity which conveniently backfilled the odd void I felt leaving the intimate world of the river and our boat. Unlike astronauts, after the Safari there isn't really a way to prepare for the somewhat awkward re-entry into the Earth's atmosphere. I felt like I had been away for ages. I was at a loss for words and simply enjoyed the steady string of hugs and accolades from family and friends.

Russell Wilde from YNN News was at the seawall steps asking for an interview. I found myself uncharacteristically blank in front of the camera. When asked how I got through the race I believe I sputtered something extraordinarily awkward like, "I just kept saying 'Seadrift! Seadrift! Seadrift!' while I was paddling."

After starting the race dead last, I was proud of the fact that we finished in the top half of the field. As pleased as I was about our finish time, the best part about arriving when we did was getting to participate in the Safari Banquet, which is held at the 75-hour mark, exactly noon on Tuesday. Winners had already been in Seadrift for over a day and couldn't be expected to wait any longer for trophies. The banquet took place under the pavilion along the seawall just yards from the finish line steps.

After running to Tom's car for a quick change into dry clothes, I joined the other racers, team captains, families, and friends for a seafood buffet, speeches, and stories of the race. Trophies were awarded to those that won their classes.

The winning team was a six-man boat that crossed the finish line at 34 hours and 40 minutes, which was just about the point when we were pulling away from the Cheapside Checkpoint north of Cuero. It was a mix of Texan and Belizean teammates, a few of which I'd had the pleasure of meeting during the months of training and preparation. I'm sure they wouldn't recall those brief encounters, but I do, because they were unceasingly courteous and supportive about my novice run at a Safari patch.

My guru John Bugge and his girlfriend Meagan won the Mixed Tandem class (the same class as Phil and me) with a finishing time of 46 hours.

My friends Debbie, Ginsie and Janie, the Hippie Chicks, won the Women's class with a finishing time of 70 hours and 29 minutes. They had been training and gunning for a faster finish but had spent the night on the bay which delayed them considerably. Earlier in the race Janie had taken ill for about 24 hours of vomiting and other gastrointestinal unpleasantness, but she kept paddling and they finished. Having also completed marathons and at least one Iron Woman competition, Janie maintains that the Safari is the hardest thing she's ever done. A two-woman novice team caught up with them and threatened to beat them for the Women's title, but The Hippie Chicks pulled it out in the end.

Tom and our chase team shared all sorts of tales they witnessed on the banks. Apparently one female paddler lost her shoe in a patch of deep, thick mud, and at one of the checkpoints her teammates helped her fashion a replacement from seat foam, Zip-ties, and duct tape. She crossed the finish line with her foam-block loafer still attached.

As teams took the stage to receive their Safari patches, there was one story after the next about trouble in the bay. Canoes swamped. Paddles floated away. Team captains were worried that their racers were stuck out there running out of food and water. Several race officials claimed definitively that these were the worst bay conditions in Safari history.

Phil asked if I wanted to say anything when we walked on stage to receive our patches, but I shook my head emphatically. I was no stranger to public speaking, but I was having an out-of-body experience there at the Seadrift Pavilion and couldn't be certain that when I went to open my mouth I wouldn't accidentally pee on myself instead. I thought it best to just get my patch and scurry back to my plate of food.

When they called our team name and finishing time it was pretty heady walking up there in front of the greater Safari community. Phil took the microphone and was gracious as he announced that we had raced to raise money and awareness for Rett Syndrome. I was touched that he took the time to promote and adopt my mission. I was thankful that he spread the word since I was suddenly mute. After our congratulatory handshake we each received our patch, along with a wooden plaque that read "Finisher Award, Texas Water Safari 2010." The plaque was a surprise, and it was nice to have a memento with the actual year listed but, honestly, it didn't carry the same iconic mystique as the patch.

It was real. It was mine. Sophie was leaping out of her seat to touch it when I sat back down. My family was laughing and cheering. I was desperate to keep my patch safe. It was as if they had just placed a swaddled newborn in my arms, I fell in love instantly. Who knew a little scrap of fabric could stir such emotion?

If a team was spotted paddling across the bay, the emcee would suspend the ceremony and the entire crowd would do a 180 to face the water and cheer for the incoming boat. Some people would stand and walk toward the seawall. It was incredibly touching.

At around 1 p.m., Team Paddlefish decided it was time to head to the hotel for some rest and hygiene. We caravanned to Falcon Point Lodge where my mom had rooms waiting for us all. It was all I had dreamed of for the previous three and a half days; big beds with clean linens, air-conditioning fully cranked, great water pressure. We even had sliding glass doors that opened to a patio and a full view of, well, the bay.

By this point my hands were swollen beyond belief. The skin was so taut it was smooth and shiny and I couldn't bend my fingers enough to remove the hair band from my braid. My dad had to cut it out with a pocket knife.

I gathered all of my nasty clothes including the shoes, and hermetically sealed them in double Ziploc bags. They would have to travel that way to Austin until we reached a washing machine. I washed off multiple times in the shower and even used antibacterial soap to make sure no wayward fungi had tried to settle a colony somewhere on my body. By the time I finished my shower, my swollen hands were pretty much useless. With my fingers extended and hands flat, I pressed my toothbrush between both palms and awkwardly brushed my teeth.

I was too excited to nap so I lay down on the bed, the comfy mosquito-free, rock free, dirt-free bed, and decided to check my phone. I almost burst into tears when I saw all the messages. Much to my surprise, tons of people had been following our SPOT Tracker! Apparently we had given more than a few people near heart attacks when they saw the little red dot stop in the middle of the night at the edge of the bay and turn back upriver. One person after the next was sharing congratulations.

My friend and original team captain, Tosh Brown had been coming in from fishing each day in Alaska and checking our progress on his laptop via the SPOT Tracker. He told me that he panicked when he saw us turn back from the bay. He had heard my back was giving me trouble and figured it must have finally given out. He sat for two hours hitting his refresh button on the laptop while we slept at the pavilion. At 11 p.m. Alaska time, the lodge generator shut down for the night and Tosh confessed that he barely slept waiting for it to come back on at 5 a.m. He was elated when he saw our little red dot moving again on his screen.

My mother's Junior League group in Nashville was also following the SPOT Tracker. My friends from college were following it. Mom-friends from Sophie's school and friends in Alabama were setting alarms to get up in the middle of the night to see if we'd finished.

Perhaps most heart warming, we had more donations during the three days we were racing that helped us reach, and exceed, my $5,000 goal for Rett Syndrome. It was cool to hit that mark while we were actually paddling in the race itself.

Voicemails, emails, text messages, Facebook posts, blog comments. I was overwhelmed by the goodness of people. Despite the fact that I had spent months writing about this race and posting about it online and coercing people to follow along, I literally could not believe everyone cared this much. It was humbling. I was literally consumed with gratitude.

Even though I had dreamed of a soft bed and air conditioning for three days, the long nap that I had also hoped for never came. After reading all of the comments and well-wishes, my mind was spinning and sleep was not an option.

That night Team Paddlefish went to a local seafood restaurant to celebrate. It was my mom and dad, Tom, Sophie, Phil, Monica and myself. I finally ordered my much-awaited glass of red wine and laughed as everyone shared stories from the race. It was fascinating to hear about it from their point of view.

My dad tried to explain how nerve-racking it was. Quite simply he broke it down for us, "My teeth are shorter."

Tom said it felt like the intensity and emotion of watching the last two minutes of a really close football game, but for 73 straight hours.

My dad then described the tension of the finish line, "Our eyes were focused off into the distance. You'd see a dot on the horizon and your heart would leap out of your chest and you couldn't take your eyes off of it. As it got closer you realized it was the team of the guy standing next to you. You were excited for him but secretly wished it was your team coming in."

My mom and Sophie had their own car and schedule during the race. They had made friends with some of the race officials and were the first among our team to learn about the poor conditions in the bay. According to my mom, Sophie took to praying over and over again that Phil and I would be okay.

As we wrapped up dinner I realized my glass of wine was still half full. As much as I had been looking forward to it, I simply couldn't stomach it. As our plates were cleared, I began feeling dizzy and a little hot. I was "bonking" again and needed to get to bed.

I was hoping to sleep much longer, but I awoke at about 5:30 a.m. on Wednesday with my hands throbbing in pain. I took Motrin and tried to fall back asleep but I couldn't stop replaying the entire race in my mind.

We enjoyed a leisurely breakfast and then lounged around the hotel for a couple of hours. Eventually we dressed, checked out and went back to the finish line to see the final racers come in. I knew full well I could have been the last person to arrive at 99.99 hours and I was adamant that I would be there to cheer for the last Safari soul to come in.

I had worn a long sundress in an effort to cover my poison

ivy, but this was a big mistake because apparently part of the fun at the finish line is comparing rashes and trying to identify their mysterious source. Most agreed that the poison ivy had come from the logjam portage below Dupont.

As the final cutoff time neared at noon on Wednesday, we heard more crazy stories from racers and officials that were waiting at the seawall for the last few finishers.

Apparently there had been quite a battle for the top slot between a few of the multi-man teams. Boats were drafting off each other and there was some gamesmanship going into critical points of the lower Guadalupe. A few teams became disoriented in Alligator Lake. Others, however, navigated it flawlessly and got a jump on close competition who wrestled with the logjam. There was a first-ever near photo finish at the steps of the seawall. A novice boat had overshot the finish line and was approaching it from the south. Another boat was coming at it from the north. They started paddling wildly trying to reach it first and worked the crowd into a frenzy as they arrived within seconds of each other.

CJ Hall, who patrols the bay in a motorboat, had some excellent accounts of bay crossings. Several teams waved him down and begged him to take them in, they wanted to quit. To which CJ replied, "Okay, no problem. But you have to fire off a flare for me to pick you up. Safari rules." Most of them felt it would take more effort than it was worth to dig a flare out from under their spray skirt, so they trudged on to the finish line.

The only boat he couldn't dissuade was a novice team who quit the race at the pier, which is at the beginning of the seawall. This was mind-boggling to everyone who heard it. They literally quit 2,000 feet from the finish line. They could have walked the 2,000 feet on the stable seawall and dragged their boat alongside in the water. But they quit. One rumor was they didn't know where the finish line actually was. Someone else claimed they knew, but they just decided they were done with this crazy race and needed to get back to get ready for work the next day.

We watched and cheered as the final boat, a solo paddler, came in at 98 hours and 54 minutes. He was the 69th boat that finished. Twenty-five teams of the 94 boats that started never reached the finish line in Seadrift.

As we piled into our cars to caravan back to Austin, it seemed odd that we'd be home in a mere three hours after spending three days to get down here. I felt like I had just experienced the enormity of Texas via time-lapse photography. The geographical journey of this race was a poetic backdrop to the personal crusade that was happening in the boat. Texas has always been in my blood, but this race offered me the opportunity to get inside its bloodstream for awhile. As we pulsed through these native rivers, born wholly in Texas and of Texas, it's as if I was feeding off its size and strength.

I am different since the Texas Water Safari. Tom is different, too. My dad has even said more than once that being a part of this race was "transformative" for him. Isn't it exciting that adventures like this lie quietly in wait all around us? Crazy crusades that inspire great expectations in the lives of otherwise ordinary people like me. The Safari tripped a wire in my soul and opened my eyes to a new way.

Not long after the race someone asked me, "So, do you feel like a real paddler now?"

"No," I replied. "But I do feel like a badass."

True paddlers are consumed with the sport year-round. They're constantly training. They subscribe to magazines. They're always looking for a new race to enter. They have an ingrained urge to trade boats, paddles, and gear. I know something of this compulsive, full-immersion, cult-like behavior because fly fishermen are just the same. At the end of the day I am a fly fisher; but for one year I was a paddler. And now I know that I can be one again if the urge resurfaces.

It is estimated that there have been roughly 4,000 Safari finishes during the 48 years of the race. With so many people repeating
the race year after year, I'm told that likely means there are only about
1,000 people with Safari patches. Mine is now framed and hanging
on the wall where it serves as a constant reminder that life's ultimate
challenges are possible, but only if you actually sign up for them.

The Texas Water Safari has confirmed what I already suspected.
Whether it's casting to a bonefish on a sandy flat in the ocean, rowing
a drift boat on a river in Montana, or paddling for my life through
the heart of Texas, my star burns brightest when I am on the water.

In the end I wasn't the fastest, I wasn't the strongest, I wasn't
the best. But I was the fastest I had ever been. I was the strongest
I had ever been. And for seventy-three hours during the heat of a
Texas summer, I was at my best.

# Epilogue

Safari stories continued to float around in the hours, days and weeks following the end of the race, and eventually I was able to account for all of the paddlers that I knew personally or met along the way.

After seeing them only once during the actual race, I was devastated to learn that my friend Eric Wilder and his race partner Dan Brennen did not finish. Eric suffered a wasp sting and a severe allergic reaction that caused his face to swell horribly. They made it as far as Gonzales before they had to bow out. After everything Eric had done to help me reach the finish line, the news of their DNF was particularly sad for me.

The Marine team in their giant 6-man aluminum canoe finished in 60 hours and 50 minutes; a phenomenal time for a heavy boat that most folks counted out before the race ever started. I was proud that we stayed with them as long as we did.

Charlie Stewart, the man who broke his rudder and repaired it with the metal door of a live trap, crossed the finish line at 76 hours.

I felt a special bond with the boats that had arrived at the bay with us during the midnight gale. As we suspected, Max and Mike had awakened early and tackled the bay head-on. They finished a half-hour before us in 38th place at 72 hours and 50 minutes. Gary and Kristin, who had bunked with us at the Holiday Inn, followed shortly in 42nd place at 74 hours and 13 minutes. Kristin was especially excited about their finishing time since they were the very last boat to finish in 2009. Jamie and Brian, who were great company and competitors, finished in 43rd place with a time of 74 hours and 16 minutes.

Everyone was relieved when Sam Hilker finally climbed the steps at 80 hours and 50 minutes. Apparently, the hopeful shortcut through Alligator Lake really waylaid her. She paddled around for hours before she finally found the main river channel again. Even with that unfortunate delay, she was the only solo woman paddler to finish the 2010 Safari.

Phil and I got together with a few other Safari finishers, including the Hippie Chicks, to celebrate a few days after we were all back in Austin. Everyone had tales to tell and poison ivy progress reports to compare.

Here's a warning to all wait staff serving a group of recent Safari racers: we *will* be pulling up our shorts and t-shirts to reveal inappropriate body parts in an effort to show off vile red rashes and we *will not* have the social graces to refrain from this practice even when you are leaning over us to deposit a bowl of queso and a basket of chips. We simply aren't rehabilitated and ready for society yet.

I was shocked at how quickly my body bounced back. My back and shoulders felt fine within a couple of days. The swelling in my hands lingered a bit longer, as did nagging pains in my left wrist and my left knee. As badly as my rear-end hurt during the second half of the race, I was certain I was doomed to spend the rest of my life like a chronic hemorrhoid patient that has to carry one of those butt pillows wherever they go. Maybe it was the excitement of the bay crossing, perhaps it was the healing properties of saltwater, but once I climbed the steps in Seadrift, the aches in my derriere completely vanished. Apparently the gluteus maximus is a highly resilient body part – or maybe it just responds well to adrenalin.

All things considered, Phil and I ran a very smooth race. No sickness, no serious injuries and no extraordinary mental collapses.

We didn't break the boat in half. Yes, we had a touch of partner tension, but it sounds like most Safari teams have to hit the reset button somewhere along the race route. Phil was strong, conservative, organized, and keenly focused throughout the race. I was lucky to have found him after the flood delay, and I would definitely race with him again.

Not long after we finished the race, I remarked to Phil, "You know, every single ounce of preparation was needed to do this. Every bit of it. Not one second was wasted."

He emphatically agreed.

The weeks and months of paddling, core training, and eating right were paramount. All of the hours analyzing charts, interviewing Safari veterans, and watching videos of past races. Ruminating over gear selection. Debating which clothing items would chafe me the least. Multiple mind-numbing trips to Lowe's and Home Depot to rig and re-rig the boat. Every bit of that was required.

While the time away from Sophie was taxing, I am so proud of her involvement, patience and support, and especially grateful for her help fundraising for Rett. At the prelim races and other mini-fundraisers, she sold cookies, brownies, fridge magnets, t-shirts (and a few things that weren't actually for sale) all for the goal of increasing our donation to Rett Syndrome. In addition, she watched me set a long-term goal and then witness the grueling months of hard work and patience required to reach it. I like that she saw me lean on friends and family for support. I like that she witnessed every aspect of teamwork and the partnership that played out between Banning and me, and then ultimately Phil and me. I also like the fact that her diet and nutrition philosophies have changed since the race. Rarely do we order dinner through the driver's side window anymore.

Several weeks after the race, I remembered the food order that Phil and I had placed with our team at Dupont. We never made it to Seadrift in the middle of the night, and I was curious what became of the meal I'd dreamed of for so many hours and miles. The image was still crystal clear: a sumptuous, steaming Italian dinner—chicken parmesan—in fact, with soft bread and a crisp salad. Immediately I called my mom and asked her what happened to my Italian food order when the bay crossing delayed our arrival into Seadrift.

"Oh…that? Well we couldn't find an Italian restaurant anywhere, so I bought an off-brand frozen lasagna at the grocery store in Seadrift."

"What did you do with it?"

"We left it in the mini-fridge at the hotel."

A month or so after the race, I was looking at my framed Texas Water Safari patch on the wall in my den. Stitched on the patch is a cartoon-like illustration depicting the devil and an alligator fighting in a canoe. Instead of a paddle, the devil has a pitchfork, and the alligator is breathing fire. Frankly it's hard to tell who's winning the battle, which seems like a fitting image to represent this race. As much as the Water Safari delivered as advertised, there is one iconic experience I feel I missed out on. I never saw an alligator during the race; never saw the floating eyeballs, the protruding nostrils, or the scaly ridged tails slicing the surface of the water.

The devil? Well, I'm pretty sure we ran into him at the logjam.

After all the excitement had died down, Tom told me about a particularly intense time for him during the Safari. As we neared the coast, Tom was on a break between checkpoints, and decided to grab something to eat at the Dairy Queen in Bloomington, a very small South Texas town just minutes from Seadrift. Coincidentally, my dad walked in to the very same Dairy Queen, and Tom saw it as a sign. He was overcome with emotion from the whole adventure and came within seconds of asking my dad for my hand in marriage over a half-pound Beltbuster burger and a basket of fries.

Two months after the race, Tom Warren proposed to me on my fortieth birthday, September 14, 2010. We were married three months later.

# Acknowledgements

This book, and my coveted Texas Water Safari patch would never have been possible without such a wonderful supporting cast. From the bottom of my heart, I am exceedingly grateful to the following people.

To Tosh Brown and Departure Publishing. It's been quite a journey and you have been there from start to finish. Thank you for helping me navigate it all. And thanks for lending us your GPS and SPOT Tracker. In retrospect, very metaphorical.

Phil Meyer, thanks for taking on a last-minute total stranger that had never paddled in a long, skinny canoe. I especially enjoyed belting out those tunes hour after hour, and I am honored to have crossed the finish line with you. I doubt there are any recording contracts in our future, but we made a damn good paddling team.

Banning Collins. Thank you for a year of training, research, adventure, laughter, portages, and shuttles. Whether it's paddling or fishing, I look forward to getting back out on the water with you.

To Monica Harmon. When it comes to serving as team captain, you set the bar. You were cool, calm and reliable—and a lovely person, to boot. Beyond the ice socks and fresh water at each checkpoint, it was your smiles and encouragement that really kept us going. My family enjoyed getting to know you on this 260-mile journey.

You're the best.

For Rancey Luce and Ella Farnum. These sweet girls touched my soul and lured me out of my comfortable, everyday life. Their smiles inspired me to tackle a number of challenges during training and the race itself. At every turn they kept pushing me down that river.

To Anna and Robin Luce. Thank you for showing us all how a family is supposed to love one another. Y'all are incredible.

Bill Farnum. Thank you for being the first to ever utter the words "Rett Syndrome" to me. I truly appreciate your courageous energy, long distance cheering and positive attitude. Not to mention the cool NIKE swag!

To all the Rett Syndrome families. I genuinely appreciate you sharing stories about your daughters and rooting so hard for Team Paddlefish. Your were an inspiration to us, throughout.

To my nutritional guru, Melissa McLean Jory. You have changed my whole relationship with food and nutrition. Sophie, Tom and I are all better, stronger, healthier people thanks to you. Viva la chia!

Thanks to Tim Cole, our traveling historian, for following Team Paddlefish and documenting the whole adventure. I am grateful for the photos, the footage and your friendship.

To the readers of my blog, *Fly Fish Chick*. This book would have never happened without your loyal interest in my writing. Thank you all for tuning in to read my stories, showing such passion for the race, and cheering us on. Your comments, emails and messages mean the world to me.

I would not have been able to survive the training, complete the race, or reach my fundraising goal without the charitable donations of both dollars and equipment from many wonderful friends, companies, and organizations. Together, we raised $5,029 for the International Rett Syndrome Foundation; a special thank you to everyone who supported our cause and helped us reach that mark.

To Ruta Maya Coffee, Fire in the Gut Performance Apparel, 1379 Sports, Gruene Outfitters, Sportsman's Finest, Alamo Flyfishers, Diane Dopson Properties, Heart of Texas Kayaks, Patagonia, Pavilion Pilates, Five Rivers Delta Safaris, and Chaco Footwear. We could have never outfitted our boat and support team without your generous contributions. Thank you!

I am blessed to have made so many new friends through the The Texas Water Safari. To Eric Wilder, John Bugge, Debbie Richardson, Janie Glos, Ginsie Stauss and West Hansen: thank you for your advice and inspiration. I enjoyed racing and training with each of you. To the organizers, board members, checkpoint volunteers, race officials, and everyone involved with the Safari, thank you for putting on such a cool event. This race is about so much more than what happens on the water for 100 hours each summer.

To my editor Dave Lawton, thank you for slugging through my typos, misspellings, flagrant overuse of capital letters and awkward grammatical mistreatments. I am grateful and impressed that you paid such close attention in your high school English class.

And finally, to Sophie, Tom, my parents, friends and family. Thank you for listening as I talked incessantly about this race for over a year. Thank you to the families who kept Sophie for so many weeknight sleepovers while I trained, to everyone who changed their plans and was flexible during the race delay, and to my friends who took time to read and comment on the working draft of this book. I love you all, and it was incredibly special to share this adventure with each of you.

Peace, love and perseverance...

*Christine*

# Sources

Brick, Michael. *In 260-Mile Texas Water Safari, Surviving Is Reward Enough.* The New York Times, May 30, 2009

Gonzales Memorial Museum
(http://www.gonzalesmemorialmuseum.com)

Gwynne, S.C. *Empire of the Summer Moon.* Scribner, 2011.

Handbook of Texas Online
(http://www.tshaonline.org/handbook/online)

Jackson, Joe. *The Thief at the End of the World.* Viking, 2008

Kimmel, Jim. *The San Marcos: A River's Story.* Texas A&M University Press, 2006

*Man-killing Water Safari.* LIFE Magazine, June 7, 1963

McCord, Marc. *Gentlemen, START YOUR PADDLES!*
(http://people.tamu.edu/~bob/history2.html)

Paddle24seven.com
(http://www.paddle24seven.com)

*Palmetto State Park.* Texas Parks & Wildlife.
(http://www.tpwd.state.tx.us/spdest/findadest/parks/palmetto/)

Texas Water Safari
(http://www.texaswatersafari.org)

*The Ten Toughest Endurance Races.* Forbes.com, May 2005

*The Texas Water Safari Is an Endurance Test for Committed Paddlers.* The New York Times, June 17, 2007